Advance Praise for
One Sunny Day

"I found Hideko Tamura Snider's remarkable book to be a beautifully written, deeply moving testament to the human spirit and the transforming power of grieving. Her account of her journey, whereby she descended into the hell of atomic holocaust and emerged into caring for cancer patients undergoing radiation, teaches us all about the gifts that can grow out of loss."

—KEN MOSES, Ph.D.
Psychologist, author, and nationally known presenter on the dynamics of grieving

"A poignant, tender story of the life and loves of a Japanese child who eventually became an American mother after losing her home and family and narrowly escaping death in the U.S. bombing of Hiroshima. Without anger or bitterness, Hideko Tamura Snider tells a compelling story of death, grief, and courage, with an optimistic message for a better future. She is remarkable and tells a story we should all read."

—CORA WEISS
International Representative, Peace Action
Vice-President, International Peace Bureau

"What a gentle and powerful narrative! One feels the loving hand of her lost mother reaching through time to comfort all of us. The author guides us, quietly and with respect, through the ghost-filled world of an innocent child impacted by the horror of Hiroshima. The timeless challenges of the lost child—traumatized by the most destructive manmade event in human history—provide opportunities for the author to teach us about family and loss, culture and change, loss and rediscovery, the malleability of the human spirit, and the costs of modern life. All people optimistic about peace on earth should read this book. But more important, all of us pessimistic about humanity should read this wise book."

—BRUCE D. PERRY, M.D., Ph.D.
Director of the Civitas Child Trauma Programs at Baylor College of Medicine and author of *Maltreated Children*

"I was deeply moved by reading this book. Hideko Tamura Snider has triumphed over the earth-shattering events that devastated her childhood."

—DR. LEO SEREN
Manhattan Project physicist who came to regret his participation in creating the atomic bomb.

"In this amazing autobiography, Hideko Tamura Snider painfully probes the depths of the abyss called Hiroshima. She has given a human face to an event that still haunts, still evokes horror."

—RONALD TAKAKI, Ph.D.
Author of *A Different Mirror* and *Hiroshima: Why America Dropped the Atomic Bomb*

"This is one of the most poignant, memorable, inspiring books I have ever read. It has taken Hideko Tamura a lifetime to battle the demons that accompanied her "survival" of the atomic bombing of Hiroshima. Her simple, elegant, powerful writing brilliantly conveys the psychological and spiritual anguish and eventual triumph of her journey and includes one of the most truly amazing love stories you will ever read."

—JOHN D. CALLAWAY
Host of "Chicago Tonight" on WTTW, Chicago Public Television, and author of the book of essays, *The Thing of It Is*

One Sunny Day

A Child's Memories of Hiroshima

Hideko Tamura Snider

Foreword by Studs Terkel

OPEN COURT
Chicago and La Salle, Illinois

Dreamcatcher

Open Court's Dreamcatcher series features personal stories
of discovery, healing, recovery, and inner development.

Open Court Trade and Academic Books is a division of Carus Publishing
Company

Copyright © 1996 by Carus Publishing Company

First printing 1996

Printed and bound in the United States of America.

Library of Congress Cataloging-in-Publication Data

Snider, Hideko Tamura, 1934–
   One sunny day: a child's Hiroshima memories / Hideko Tamura
Snider.
      p.   cm.
   Includes index.
   ISBN 0-8126-9327-2 (paper: alk. paper)
   1. Hiroshima-shi (Japan)—History—Bombardment, 1945—Personal
narratives. 2. World War, 1939–1945—Children—Japan—Hiroshima-
shi. 3. Snider, Hideko Tamura, 1934–. 4. Atomic bomb victims—
Japan—Hiroshima-shi—Biography. 5 Girls—Japan—Hiroshima-
shi—Biography. I. Title
D767.25.H6S56 1996
940.53'161—dc20   96-18268

For All that teaches us to become truly human

Contents

Foreword

Was it the afternoon of August 6, 1945 or was it evening that I heard of IT? A single bomb that would incinerate more people than a hundred of the usual such killers? It worked. The scientists at Alamagordo, our most brilliant, came through.

As Philip Morrison remembers—he was a nuclear physicist at the time, working in the desert: "What can we do to end this war? The army said we'll give you the wonderful opportunity to make the world's greatest explosion and all you have to forget, it's going to make a bomb that will kill very many people. A Faustian bargain."

And the light of a thousand suns bewitched Hiroshima.

What happened three days later, a like one, wholly gratuitous it appears, was dropped over Nagasaki. I guess it was to prove that the first was not simply a matter of luck, a chancy success.

It was the news from Hiroshima, though, that caused the astonishment. And in most instances, on these shores, elation. There were some few who were distraught; the Quakers, of course, among them. I'm ashamed to say I was not among these few. It was later . . .

What Wilfred Owen called Chance's strange arithmetic was at work. I was a thirty-three-year-old radio commentator in Chicago; Hideko Tamura was a little school girl in Hiroshima.

As she recalls in her achingly moving memoir a half century later: "A typical summer day was about to begin with a gentle breeze on my face and bare back and I wore just my underpants. I was very relaxed when the air raid warning siren went off around 7:15 A.M. . . . A casual warning was being issued: three enemy planes were en route. 'Only three?' I shrugged. It was hardly worth being warned about. Hundreds maybe, but three?

"A little later around 7:30 A.M., the simple announcement came that the planes had turned around. The warning was off. I heard Aunt Fumiko say: 'Hideko it's so nice out.'"

Then came the blinding flash and the white light. And the rest, as they say, is history.

Unfortunately, history does not recount a small girl's search for her elegant young mother, who loved Tolstoy and Wordsworth, buried somewhere in the rubble. And crying out that soft song her mother used to sing. Nor does it tell us of a teenaged American POW, standing numb and naked in the deracinated village square, about to be stoned by grief-maddened, wounded old men and women, and saved by her father, an army officer. Talk about Chance's strange arithmetic.

There have been scores of such remembrances recorded, but few that so touch and sear the soul as much as this childhood memory of one sunny day.

STUDS TERKEL

Acknowledgments

This book was written originally out of a mother's wish to chronicle the heritage of her past for her daughter and son. The encouragement to turn it into a publication came from a small group of amateur writers in a western suburb of Chicago. I owe a special debt to Dr. Samuel Hellman of the University of Chicago Hospitals and Michael Moore of the *Bulletin of the Atomic Scientists* whose decision to publish an abridged version of the early chapters of this work spurred interest in publication by the present publisher.

Many persons extended generous help before the manuscript was finalized. My children, Miko and Joshua, were the first to give feedback and suggestions. My friends and neighbors, Betty and Frances Clegg, were invaluable supporters before my husband, Robert, arrived from Alaska. His editorial and moral support were relied on heavily throughout.

The work's photographic section could not have been completed without the generous cooperation of the senior librarian of the East Asian Library of the University of Chicago, Mr. Eizaburo Okuizumi, whose support and encouragement have been deeply appreciated.

Finally, my editor, Kerri Mommer, has been a steady source of patient assistance at all times enabling me to do my best. To all of these individuals I am greatly in debt.

Introduction

Every year when the days begin to stretch and the penetrating heat of summer rises to a scorching point, I am brought back to one sunny day in a faraway land. I was a young child, waiting for my mother to come home. On that day, however, the sun and the earth melted together. My mother would not come home. On that day she became a statistic along with many of my relatives, neighbors, and my best friend.

Just the day before, my best friend Miyoshi and I had returned to Hiroshima from a remote village to which we had been evacuated. Our mothers would have preferred resting a day before going back to Hiroshima, but we children could not wait to get home after months of starvation and labor. Miyoshi was headed to her grandparents' home, near the center of Hiroshima. We said good-bye, promising to see each other soon.

The long journey after that one sunny day was a lonely trek for those of us who survived. There were no trodden paths or road signs pointing to our destiny ahead. Our ability to feel became compromised by a transparent wall of desensitization, but it was not enough to keep out the memory of the abyss and its crippling consequences.

And yet, there were moments from time to time when we recognized the enormity of our experiences and were able to be whole again. One such moment came to my father and me more than twenty-three years after the bombing, when he traveled to be at my wedding ceremony in Chicago. Remembering the unspeakable past, he shared something he had never told anyone before.

He spoke of encountering a young American prisoner of war surrounded by a crowd of injured civilians, a few hours after the A-bomb explosion. The young man, no more than seventeen, with blond hair and blue eyes, was naked, with the exception of his boxer shorts. My father was shocked to see the crowd of mostly old men and women, carrying stones to take on the wanderer. My father, in his role as a military officer, intervened, reproaching these otherwise ordinary and peaceful citizens by pointing out that the unarmed young man, as a prisoner under the protection of the military, was obviously not about to harm them, adding that they must not become killers themselves.

Later, it was learned that the bomb had killed some forty to fifty American prisoners who were located near the epicenter. My father, who was in charge of the clearing task force, was asked if the bodies of the prisoners should be cremated along with the Japanese. He told the workers that the American soldiers should be granted their own country's custom, which was to be buried. By the banks of the Ota River, then, the Americans who perished in Hiroshima were buried. He said he often wondered long after the war about the handsome young man with fearful eyes, and about his parents. They must have wondered about their son who never came home. I was stunned. There were tears in our eyes.

Who could have known that the fate of Americans was sealed with ours? Our fate was joined, even then.

Somehow, I had known this all along from my mother, a woman who loved Tolstoy and Wordsworth, singing songs of spring to her little girl in the depths of winter. Melodies of East and West lingered in my ears, gently hummed by a young, loving woman.

Over fifty years have passed. What was lost then could not be brought back except in my memories. I wish you could have been there before the destruction. I wish you could have met my young mother who, though this was unrecognized except by her daughter, was indeed a "universal" woman. If you had, you would have missed her profoundly, as I do.

I was born to parents who defied tradition and married out of deep love for each other at a time when such actions were unthinkable. Fate, also married to us, had brought forth the unthinkable. My mother and I would not have been in Hiroshima if my father had not had to leave us because of the war. We would not have moved to Hiroshima.

On one sunny day, my world and the young woman for whom my father had sacrificed everything disappeared from the face of this earth. This is the story of my childhood during wartime, and my struggle to reconnect and find meaning in the absurd reality of my time. This search eventually led to an ocean voyage that brought me to the shores of the very country which had bombed my hometown, years before.

Won't you journey with me as I look back one more time?

1

In the Beginning

Sunken stone steps, sandwiched between wooden fences and white walls, were unevenly paved in a quaint alley in a corner of Tokyo. It was a narrow walkway that led to my parents' little house and garden. The intricately laid out garden included a small pond, shaded by evergreens and a few large granite rocks of different shapes resting around it. The rocks were perfect for hiding behind, jumping off of, and sliding down before I discovered the school playground.

Butterflies and insects also found respite there during spring and long summers. I would know. Trying to step into my father's large garden *getta* sandals one morning, I was stung by a live bee that I did not see under my foot. The mighty sting prompted a hearty yell and an early lesson in life that even a child must first look before she steps.

On rainy days, jumping out from under the rocks and tree bases, frogs hopped from one puddle to another in the garden. Holding an umbrella, I used to crouch in the rain and watch these creatures like a kitten watching fish in a pond. My early world was filled with an endless array of objects to be discovered and observed.

Our little house had other essentials. The guest room, called the *zashiki,* was the largest room. It faced our tranquil garden. A wooden corridor next to the guest room led to the toilet area, separated from the living quarters. It was poorly lit and was the only scary place in the house. We used specially designated slippers for entry there. I refused to go there alone, unless my mother would call my name loud enough, so as to be heard, and could come running if anything happened. It was a bit of a nuisance for both of us.

In a small room behind the guest room, there was a Western-style bed where my parents slept. They did not use a futon or sleep on a *tatami* mat. There was an oversized reed cradle which was mine. I assume it was oversized, since I remember crawling into it until my fourth or fifth birthday.

Adjoining the bedroom was a small dining area and kitchen where my mother spent many hours preparing meals and snacks. Our breakfasts were seldom the traditional Miso soup and rice, but more often toast and pancakes with eggs, sometimes even with bacon. My mother prepared mostly Western dishes, quite different from the meals my maternal grandmother used to cook whenever we visited. I liked both kinds of food.

My father, Jiro Tamura, was a young Keio graduate, but simply "Papa" to me. Papa majored in law as his elder brother before him had. He was the second son of the founder of the Tamura Industrial Group, which led the industrialization of Hiroshima. The company produced needles and rubber goods, conducted sales operations across Japan, and ran overseas branches in China and Manchuria.

Papa had thick, dark brown, curly hair, making him look quite like the painter he had always wanted to be. He was short but average height for his generation, with a wiry frame. He was a powerful swimmer, and his sturdy shoulders gave me a great vantage point as he would hoist me up while strolling or browsing through the *yomises'* (night vendors') displays on evenings after supper.

My aunts and uncles told me that my parents met at an annual baseball pennant game between Keio and Waseda Universities. After Papa saw my mother and my aunt in the spectators' stand, he followed them home. He asked my grandmother for permission to court Mama, and was flatly turned down. It would not have been proper for Mama or her mother to have accepted such a bold request by a young man without even a proper introduction by a "go-between," usually a respectable elder or a relative. In those days, people married by arrangement, without courtship. All mixing of the sexes was chaperoned very closely by the elders. Papa refused to give up his interest in Mama, however, and eventually gained permission to court her.

Papa's family strongly objected to the marriage. They had planned to choose Papa's bride just as they had done for his elder brother. Marriages were arranged between the families of social and financial equals, and definitely not between young lovers. A young woman from a family headed by a widow with a limited financial allowance was definitely not their idea of a suitable match for the second son of the Tamura Industrial Group.

Neither Papa nor his family gave in. His actions eventually resulted in his expulsion from his family in Hiroshima. This meant he would receive no more financial support from them. For the first time in his life, Papa went to work to support himself and his family.

During the week, he worked for Nissan Motors as a salesman. At a time when driving was only for the privileged, he drove a Datsun home on many evenings. His friends from work and from his university days flocked to our house. Nabe-san from Nissan, Ryochan from Takashimaya, and Ina-san, have all gone on to take prominent places in their fields. I can still hear their hearty laughter, their clapping hands, and their singing late into the night, as they feasted on food prepared by Mama.

Painting was Papa's hobby, and quite a serious one. Initially, he had wanted to attend the prestigious Tokyo Art Institute instead of Keio University, but his wish was denied by his parents who did not consider a career in art to be a very substantial profession for a man.

After his break from the family, Papa often painted for long hours. He wore a smock and worked with great concentration. We did not interrupt. We knew better. He would not have heard us anyway. Sometimes he asked me to sit as his subject, but I could never be still long enough.

I can almost smell the paint today as I recall his paintings. They were painted in soft colors, highlighting the presence of light in his imagination. They were very different from the photographic paintings of that time. Sometimes, he taught me how to make drawings in perspective, and how to paint with a sense of light. I understood later that he admired the French Impressionists. His favorite painter was Cezanne.

Papa was a quiet man, and there was a flowing rhythm of affability about him. His face broke into soft, carefree smiles when he was around family and friends. After the war when my mother was gone, however, I seldom saw his wonderful smiles.

My mother, Kimiko Kamiya, was "Mama" to her little daughter, never *Oka-san* (mother), what other children called their mothers. After passing a formidable entrance examination, she attended Daisan Women's School. She was planning to be a school teacher, but her father Toshi's sudden illness and death, from complications of pneumonia, changed the course of her life. Mama was the oldest of six, with four sisters and one brother. They had all enjoyed a comfortable middle-class Japanese home life up until that time.

Grandfather Toshi was a sibling partner in a large real-estate holding company in an elite residential section of Tokyo called Kojimachi. His brothers, however, took over the estate without adequately providing for the widow and her children. Grandmother Tome and the six children were moved into small quarters and given a limited allowance.

One day, Mama was called before her uncle and told that she could not continue her schooling. The money saved was to go into the family allowance. Mama had to give up her Daisan uniform and find a job to help the family. It was at this time that she was forced to abandon the traditional dependence on male elders, taking on independence and self support. She became a modern girl from this point on.

Mama was slender in build and tall for a Japanese woman. Her large, expressive eyes, long thick eyelashes, and well defined eyebrows were not typical Japanese features. I remember how striking she used to look when she dressed up, and how people's heads turned when she walked down the street. Most of the time, she chose Western clothes with hats and heels over kimonos and *obis*. Mama once told me that she had been approached by movie producers for movie parts, but she declined. My neighboring friends used to tell me how lucky I was to have such a pretty mother.

Mama spoke in a soft and gentle voice. She had a demure presence. However, she was as firm as steel inside. Once Mama made up her mind, she was not easily swayed. "No" meant no, and "yes" was yes with my mother, regardless of how she may have seemed on the outside. At times, this quality of hers had shocked others who least expected such strength from one so soft and frail in appearance.

Like other Japanese mothers, she was always busy cooking, sewing, knitting, and housecleaning. She made all my clothes, and was a speedy knitter. My sweaters and leggings had beautiful geometrical designs that she made up. I can still see them before my eyes. At the same time, she made everything seem effortless, whether making dolls or teaching me how to fold an origami ghost on a rainy day. Step by step, she took me through the intricate folding process with the simple square papers. It was like magic.

In my later years when I saw the movie *The King and I*, I was reminded of Mama's love of singing. Like Anna, she shared her open spirit with others by reaching out and singing. Her voice was soft and tender, just like her speaking voice, humming tunes new and old, Scottish, Irish, German, French, Italian, Russian, and, of course, Japanese. Sometimes Mama would make hand and body motions like a singer, which I would imitate, and we would sing song after song together.

A song I used to ask her to sing, time and again, was a melody for springtime. It was a song from a Takarazuca musical, set in a European village. The vibrant and upbeat rhythm was perfect for Mama, and for singing in the middle of a cold and dreary winter while we waited for the arrival of springtime.

My parents had a large bookcase filled with their books. The bottom shelf, however, was stocked with my storybooks. More than half of my books were stories of faraway lands. Andersen and Aesop's fables were read to me just as often as the beloved Japanese fables. Fairy tales of kings, queens, and princesses, from *Snow White*, *Sleeping Beauty*, and *Cinderella*, to *Hansel and Gretel*, came into my world just as early in my childhood as any small child born in the Western world would have encountered them. *Robinson Crusoe, Tom Sawyer, Huckleberry Finn, The Little Prince* and *The Little Princess*, or even *Uncle Tom's Cabin* and *Robinhood* were all on that bottom shelf.

There was also children's poetry by Hakushu Kitahara among others, which brought a sense of pathos and mystery into life. These poems were presented without moral teachings and obvious solutions. Mama must have been partial to those themes.

Sunday was usually saved for the family, having Mama's sisters and my favorite, Uncle I-chan, come and visit us. Sometimes we would all go out to the Ueno Zoo or the amusement park, Toshima-waen. We were poor then compared to the standards of my later life but I think that my parents had just as good a time in these outings as I did. We laughed, strolled, and played games until we were exhausted and ready to come home.

There were other exciting things like the Celestial Festival in early July and the Fall Festival for the Hie-shrine every autumn. The star studded sky above the tall evergreens and the Gingko trees would be lit up in colorful fireworks, while the merchants lined the street with their goods. People in *yukata*, fanning themselves as they walked, would fill the streets on the festival night.

Being expelled from the family was more like a liberation for Papa. His family ties to his father and his elder brother were unbroken. We saw my soft-spoken and generous *ojii-chan* (grandfather) every few months. The announcement of his arrival at the *genkan* entrance signaled excitement and joy in the family.

He brought gifts of candy, toys, and food. I would climb on his lap, and he would read to me. Soon, Grandpa would feign a sore shoulder, wondering if anyone could make his shoulder feel better. I would volunteer to give special shoulder rubs and tapping for which he would announce I was the best granddaughter in all of Japan. His encouragement usually prompted more back rubs. A clever grandfather he was.

His soothing voice and tranquil presence was like warm sunshine. The next day, he would take us to some of our favorite shops in downtown Tokyo. Mine was an elegant fruit-parlor called Senbikiya for a chocolate parfait. Papa's elder brother also came along on regular visits to us and to Senbikiya.

The only issue about which my parents disagreed in my presence was how to descipline me when I was out of line for one thing or another. Papa's method was a threat of *okyu*, moss-burning on the skin, a home remedy usually tried by adults for a persistent ailment, but sometimes used for punishing incorrigible children. Always believing his threats, Mama pleaded with him that a skin of a girl child must not be scarred. Papa, a nontraditional man, stopped short each time in response to this traditional plea. I always wailed, just in case he was serious.

But a more effective discipline came from a different source. I was afraid of street monks. They wore reed headgear that covered their faces when they came to our houses. Like the dark bathrooms, I did not take to anyone or anything I could not see plainly. Even a hint of a monk near the house was enough to prompt immediate obedience. It became a joke for my parents to see me reverse my behavior from "no" to a sudden "yes," just because I thought a monk was at our door. Bathing in peach leaf water to cure a summer rash was one of those occasions when I had to be persuaded. Nothing else could make me jump in a tub full of smelly green leaves.

I felt the same way towards studio photographers. Facing a man with a flashing bright light who was hiding under a dark cloth and behind a three-legged box was no occasion for me to smile. In one of my rare official photos of this period, I was shown seated on a bench with a forlorn teddy bear thrown on the opposite side, hinting at the foregone struggle.

These were the days of my early life, when I was nurtured by parents who sought the freedom to choose their own partners and to raise their "child of love" in a tradition of their own.

2

Changing World

One day I found Mama sitting down, looking worried. She had her face covered. Mama was not the worrying kind. She hesitated to explain, as though she was at a loss for words. Again, this was not my Mama. When Papa returned home, they locked the *amado*, the rain door, which is usually only done at night before going to bed. I was sent away to my bedroom, while they discussed the problem in the *zashiki*. It must have been a wrenching argument for shouting and pleading went on for quite some time. The next day, Mama went to talk with a friend of my father, Ryo-chan, and left me with my Uncle, I-chan. As he was closer to my age than my mother's other siblings, Uncle I-chan grew up with me. We had played together. He was resourceful and observant, so I was sure he knew what was going on.

Uncle I-chan was tentative in his reply as I persisted in trying to find out what was happening. He thought that we might have to move, because the red paper had come to Papa, which meant that he was being drafted into the Imperial Army. The argument be-tween my parents had ensued because Papa wanted to send his wife and child to Hiroshima, while Mama refused to comply. She preferred staying with her own mother in Tokyo.

What could have persuaded Mama to change her mind is still a mystery. Within a short time, we closed up our little house and boarded a train, riding towards Papa's home from which he had been expelled. He was now returning with his wife and child to attempt a formal reconciliation. He must have loved us profoundly to have undertaken such an awesome task to assure our legal protection in the possible event of his demise on the battlefield. In objecting to this plan, Mama, strong as she was, must have also sensed the enormity of the uphill struggle this change would bring for her.

My first railway trip spanned half the main island of Japan, Honshu, from Tokyo to Hiroshima. We rode all day and all night. At stops, *bento* lunches, tea, and cakes were being sold by tireless venders bellowing out their specialties while walking up and down the platforms. One had to choose and transact with lightning speed, for half of one's change and food might miss one's outstretched hand. Rivers and mountains passed behind us at times quickly and at times slowly. The worst thing I would encounter was an unexpected cinder in my eye when the train went into a tunnel with the window open. The smell and the soot particles flew into the cabin, covering my face and hair. This was not a time of clean air.

In Hiroshima, we were first taken to the house of grandfather's eldest daughter by his first marriage, Aunt Chitose, and her husband, Tokuichi. Their two-story house was built on a river bank and one could actually step into the cool, clear water of the Ota River from the yard. Aunt Chitose, who resembled a picture of a celestial fairy out of my storybooks, delicate and fair, was awaiting our arrival. She and Uncle Tokuichi welcomed us as if we were already family. Their two young sons, Hiroshi and Shoji, clean-cut and shy, joined in the solicitude. We were to wait at this house while the members of my father's family formally negotiated the terms of our re-entry into the family. Trying to keep me occupied, Aunt Chitose used to take me to the upper floor, which opened to a deck where she hung her laundry out to dry. One could see not only the flowing river, but also the graceful Hiroshima Castle and other houses along the river. At night, a long array of lights was reflected in the water, moving with the wind tide. I had never seen such beauty. Like the gondolas in Venice, ferries and pleasure boats passed by day and night. This was a Venice of the Orient, the castle town of Hiroshima.

As expected, my Papa's wish for us to live under the same roof with his family was met with some resistance, but was ultimately approved by the family council at which grandfather presided. I never doubted that he was anxious to have us close by. We moved on with blessings from our hosts to the grand estate of Hidetaro Tamura, my grandfather and chairman of the Tamura Industrial Group. Mama wore a new kimono in yellow and blue with a light green *haori* coat, a gift from her new in-laws. I wore my gold and white knit pants and a dress set made by Mama.

The estate was built several feet above the ground, with layers of large rocks at the base fashioned after old castles. From the base stood long white walls with a tile roof at the top circling the outside perimeter. Impressive ironwork adorned the main gate which stood at the entrance to a wide marble driveway. The side entrance was large enough to fit a tiny house through, and was used more frequently. We were ushered through this entrance, greeted by a line of white-aproned women and two men whom I recognized from our previous friendly visits. Strangely, I was not to mention these prior contacts in the presence of the rest of the family. The complexity of the necessary discretion was beyond anyone unfamiliar with the "politics" of family tradition. Such complexities began to unfold after Papa was formally inducted into the army and later sent to Northern China.

The first morning in the new house came early, as I woke to sounds of voices and footsteps. I ventured out to explore, prancing down the long corridor, and upon hearing a child's voice, I peeked inside a room. These were Uncle Hisao's living quarters. His only son, Hideyuki, was just getting his shirt on with the help of his mother, Fumiko. She was surprised to see me but quickly invited me to come in and sit with cousin Hideyuki. I recognized a familiar book cover, so I took it to my startled cousin, and offered to read with him. He kept very quiet, while I read it with much drama. This episode became legendary as I learned later. This became the tale of the little girl who was more outgoing than anyone who had ever been seen.

At the end of an almost endless corridor was a large dressing room with a giant wall mirror. I gasped, seeing a very strange phenomenon. A creature with no hair was seated before a three-dimensional vanity. Several women were fussing, combing, and painting white liquid from the neck up. The illustration from one of my storybooks labeled "A sea monster" loomed into my mind at that instant. On the verge of terror, I hurried back to my room, wasting no time reporting the discovery to Mama. Seeing that I was truly serious, she stopped laughing, and in a hushed voice deciphered the mystery. I was dumbfounded. She explained that the person was Grandmother Tamano. By the time I returned to the scene, a new set of hair covered her head. More make-up was being applied by the same attendants who now assisted in robing her in a kimono. I was being introduced to some of the household's morning rituals.

There were other activities entirely new to me. Before our breakfast, freshly cooked rice was served at the Grand Buddhist altar. Incense was burned, a gong struck, and the morning sutra chanted. The room-sized altar was in a large black lacquer case, which could open and close. The room was called the *butsuma*, the place of Buddha. We congregated there in the evening for still longer worship services that were conducted by Grandfather. After the sutra chanting, he would read from the holy text during which time our heads were bowed down to the *tatami* floor showing humility and reverence. Mama instructed me now simply to do as I was told without asking any questions. I did so, almost for the first time, but this was a very necessary change, indeed. After a while, I began to memorize the words and chanted in unison with the others. This family took their customs seriously, and this was by far the most solemn occasion.

The entire household came together at mealtimes. We ate in a large dining room next to an even larger kitchen. As the days of toast with bacon and eggs were gone, we now ate only rice, fish, and vegetables. Grandfather sat at the head of the table, sipping his ceremonial morning tea, followed by carrot juice or miso soup, *daikonoroshi*, grated white radish, and pickles and rice. Uncle Hisao and Cousin Hideyuki sat on one side, and Papa and I sat on the other side of the table. Grandmother was usually at the end of the table, opposite grandfather. Aunt Kiyoko, father's oldest sister, divorced by her husband and childless, sat next to Grandmother.

Mama and Aunt Fumiko were kept busy and ate next to the last. The last of the crew were three maids and little Auntie Kimie, who I learned long afterwards was grandfather's daughter by his first wife who had died. It was generally a happy time, but I had to be careful not to make any references to wonderful prior visits with the men of the family. Once I almost forgot. I started to say something, but was caught by a sudden pain in my toes tucked under my bottom on the *tatami* floor. Mama was pinching me.

Most of my daytime hours were spent playing with Cousin Hideyuki, who became my only brother in residence. Though lacking in urban experiences, he was a master climber, catcher of insects, and an excellent player of marbles and paper *pachinko*. I learned and practiced all of his crafts so that we could play together. He loved having a playmate. Sometimes he made me cry during fights, though not often. Aunt Fumiko always stopped her son from being rough with me and apologized on his behalf.

When Cousin Hideyuki was otherwise occupied, the vast garden of the estate was at my disposal for endless pleasure. There were about five or six gardens in various sections inside the wall, each meticulously maintained. There were beautifully shaped pine trees, well placed giant rocks, and stone lanterns. Large azalea bushes, flowering trees, evergreens, and maple trees were laid out in such a way one was awed by the beauty from any vantage point in the garden all year around. In the winter, the camellias bloomed in bright red, pink, and white, next to shiny green holly leaves with red berries. Early spring brought azaleas of every color as well as golden and silver lilacs that filled the air with their wonderful aroma. Herbs and other condiment plants grew in shady spots, and a small orchard across the formal estate produced figs and persimmons galore. Cousin Hideyuki and I feasted on the fruits even before the picking time.

Besides birds and insects, there was a variety of stunning colored lizards and large ground frogs. These were not like the little jumping wet frogs I enjoyed in my parents' garden in Tokyo. They were huge, covered with unsightly warts, but harmless. On rare occasions I also saw a white snake going across a pond. It was an awesome sight to see a long, stringlike creature crossing the water effortlessly.

Although my life was changed drastically in many ways after the move, it was nothing compared to the changes my mother endured. She went from being a carefree young wife and mother to being a member of a large, structured household, responsible for an army of chores and governed by countless rules. This must have been extremely difficult for someone accustomed to being mistress of her own household for so long. Aunt Fumiko, Mama, Auntie Kimie, and the maids were up at the crack of dawn, washing the floors, sweeping entrance ways as well as preparing breakfast. The continuous work did not end until long after dark.

Grandmother and Aunt Kiyoko made decisions, organized the chores, and supervised their performance. The standards were high, and the women were kept on their toes. The hardest part of my adjustment was the loss of my mother's company. Our private time together was mostly at bedtime, unless I became ill, or she disobeyed.

Shortly after our arrival, Papa was inducted into the military. After basic training, he was assigned to the transport division because of his driving experience from the Nissan days. We were secretly delighted that he had not been assigned to the infantry, in spite of the patriotic fervor of the time. Within six months, his division had received orders to go to Northern China.

On the morning of Papa's departure, the entire Tamura clan was gathered at the Ujina harbor with a spread of festive foods and sake bottles. Grandfather's siblings and the household, and Papa's married sisters and their children were all present. Decanters were filled and emptied quickly. Men were singing send-off songs and women were busy filling the plates for the men. There was nothing festive about this event for me. I was losing my Papa. No one seemed grievous. They were congratulating the man who was going to serve his country for his Emperor.

I remember being very thirsty and reaching for the nearest tea cup. Drinking it hastily, I realized later that it was filled with rice wine. I had not tasted an alcoholic beverage before. It was too late. I finished the cup, and helped myself to more. No one realized what had happened until I began to sing and dance, circling a telephone pole. A few of my male cousins were amused when they guessed what had happened. An intoxicated child saw off her father in khaki uniform. His curly hair had been shaved off. Looking very much like a soldier, he gave a military salute to his family before boarding a small ferry with other inducted men. Everyone was calling out the last well wishes and good-byes. I shouted a wish for a letter and watched him become a pinpoint on the horizon.

I looked for Mama, and cried out, calling for her help. A change of diet, together with a few helpings of sake, was beginning to cause a giant stomach ache. Mama tried to comfort me, but she, too, was weeping. We walked along together, feeling very tired and lost, towards our uncertain future without Papa.

3

Becoming a Tamura

The days that followed our good-byes to Papa were eventful. Since I had just turned five, I was to participate in the religious ceremony called "seven-five-three" at the temple. The ceremony was an official act of welcoming the children to the Buddhist family. Cousin Hideyuki and I paraded in ceremonial costumes, carrying ornamental water lilies and bells, wearing delicate golden tresses on our heads. It was a ritual of dedication, in the presence of the temple family, called, "Tokuoji, The Temple of the Virtuous King." I remember crying and not wanting to be paraded around or to have my face painted white. I felt like a clown. This was an important occasion, however, in which a child had little choice of her own. We walked in a circle on the temple stage, around and around, cheered on by our proud parents.

Another formal initiation into the tradition of the Tamura family included attendance at the Seibi Academy sponsored by Kaiko-sha, a powerful, educational auxiliary of the Japanese military. It was a private academy for the children of the elite of Hiroshima. Both

Uncle Hisao and Papa had graduated from this school, and some of their teachers were still on the faculty.

My first attendance was informal. Aunt Fumiko had taken me along on Cousin Hideyuki's first day of school. Mr. Sato, the teacher, opened the class by asking easy questions like the ages of his young students, "How many here are six . . . ? and how many seven . . . ?" Eager children were raising their hands. "Is there anyone five?" Way in the back, sitting with the parents, a lone hand went up, mine. Mr. Sato was hesitant, clearing his throat, but finally saying, "Of course, class, you are not five." I could hardly wait to be admitted.

To enter the kindergarten, as well as the first grade, the entrance examination had to be passed. A couple of kindly teachers asked questions about colors, animals, and numbers that I had to identify by moving colored beads. It was almost too easy.

The kindergarten was divided into three classrooms with names of flowers. The teachers were clad in beautiful *hakama* wear. They seemed hesitant to give quick answers or intervene. They were always sought after by the children, who pulled them from all directions. I never could find a spot to grab, so I watched from close by with envy.

Sometime during this period, Mama decided to take a short leave from the entire household and to return to Tokyo. It seemed as if she had had more than she could handle. Perhaps the decision for her to do so had not been approved by the household, for she was not allowed to take me with her. The short period of her temporary absence was devastating. When she returned after a month, I made her promise never to leave again. She kept her promise as long as she lived. In looking back, my reticence in reaching out to the teachers might have been the very time of her absence, for I was by nature a confident and outgoing child, and would normally have found a way to speak to them without any fear of rejection.

On her return, Mama was given more leeway in tending to the care and protection of her daughter. She traveled with me to school and back every day. Aunt Fumiko took Cousin Hideyuki, so the four of us now had a group outing every day. It brought our two families so close that our mothers became sisters and my cousin and I became siblings. Mama introduced her new sister to foreign cuisines at a popular restaurant in downtown Hiroshima. Spaghetti, hot dogs, and pancakes were our favorite foods. Cousin Hideyuki would always drown the pancakes in syrup. I had to show him how to melt the butter first, tucking it between the pancakes.

We learned about Aunt Fumiko's feelings under her dutiful exterior. Her mother had passed away before she married. Her father's new wife and Grandmother were friends, and they arranged Aunt Fumiko's marriage without her input. When she saw Uncle Hisao for the first time at her wedding, she wanted to cry. She said she had not favored a man with spectacles. How silly, she laughed, as she came to realize that her husband was a good man. We laughed, too.

Aunt Fumiko's endearment to Mama brought Uncle Hisao under Mama's influence. They were all delighted with Mama's lessons in ballroom dancing. Uncle Hisao had wanted to be able to dance just like his younger brother, and now, they learned as a pair. Just how and when to learn, however, were tricky things to arrange under the roof of this traditional household. We had a portable phonograph, the kind that was hand cranked before it played. It was taken to a far corner of the main corridor, which had a smooth floor surface. After the lights were out and all was quiet, the three adults tried out the steps of the fox trot, tango, and waltz with the music at the softest volume.

While our most conservative members of the household fell into slumber, a pair of most unlikely subversives were taking lessons from Mama. My uncle, a spectacled traditional gentleman, and my aunt, a model daughter-in-law, danced in each other's arms just as free in spirit as my parents had been in Tokyo. Once or twice the dancing woke others, and the phonograph was then taken away. In the following spring, the couple's only daughter, Kumiko, was born, ten years after the birth of their first child, Hideyuki.

Other delights for Mama and me came unexpectedly after I

suffered from complications of stomach troubles. I had eaten bananas from the newly acquired territories in the South Seas. A low grade fever persisted for which every home remedy was tried and failed. Finally, Aunt Chitose suggested that we see a pediatrician a few doors down from her house. He decided to try regular shots of vitamin B for a cure. Mama and I began making the trip, delighting mostly in seeing Aunt Chitose again, not for those shots that burned my skin. Cousins Hiroshi and Shoji took me to the sandy Ota River, just down the steps below the house for clam digging, shrimp scooping, and boat rides. Their bookshelf was a treasure chest of still more books and I devoured them. The visits were a time of renewal for both my mother and me.

Another accidental gift came when the bath facility had to be repaired and remodeled. The bathtub room was out of commission. Everyone had to wash in make-shift fashion unless one chose to bathe publicly at a bathhouse. No one cared to do so but Mama and me. We were a pair of *Edokko*, Tokyo-ites, sworn to be the cleanest of all. We walked to the bathhouse just around the block, carrying our own towels and soap in a little bowl. We felt relaxed and refreshed afterwards. Our short walk back home was a sheer pleasure. We sang, and looked up to the starry sky, where Mama identified constellations for me. My teacher was at work and feeling well.

Meanwhile, Papa kept his promise of writing to us often. We sent letters filled with news, with many pictures that I drew just for him. The *imon bukuro* (care packages) were sent just as often. Mama wrote, asking for his permission to visit her family in Tokyo, taking me with her. He consented and asked his family to allow our trip. His peace of mind while serving the Emperor was important enough for the family to go along. Mama and I began to make the long train rides back and forth to Tokyo during all my long school holidays. I even spent a little period in second grade at the Nagata-cho Grade School by the Diet building in Tokyo, following a long siege of the whooping cough.

One day in early spring, Papa returned from China just as suddenly as he had left three years before. He was full of colorful tales from his tour of duty. Everything was recorded in a couple of thick black and white photo albums that he kept. The vast deserts of China and Manchuria, and people in their native garb, now looked into our eyes from a faraway tiny country. Papa showed us their artifacts as well. The most impressive of these were Mongolian utensils: an awesome cutting knife and long chopsticks that were held in an intricately decorated case. He told me that such utensils were carried by the Mongolian nomads everywhere. I imagined the sharp blades plunging into things as I fantasized about the conquest of Gengis Khan and the Silk Road. The history and the stories I read were coming to life. I hoped to see such a land some day.

He also talked about his delight in finding simple and inexpensive cures for sick natives with stomach problems. The army doctors could dispense powders from broken clay roof tiles. It made him feel better to aid the suffering. There was an expression of genuine relief and a smile on his face as he talked about it. He also recalled how he had never seen anywhere else the vast level of poverty in the streets, and such a difference between the rich and the poor. He was amazed they coexisted. In my child's mind I gathered from his description that in China there was a huge number of poor people ruled by a small number of very wealthy people.

I felt a bit shy when I first saw Papa. It was like getting to know one another all over again, perhaps even more so for him, as I had grown and changed. I wanted to tell him all that had happened, but found myself tongue tied and couldn't. I was no longer the bubbly child he had left behind. We did manage to find our way back to each other in time. He had seen and lived a very different life in the three years he was gone. I did not know how his experiences in those years might have changed him, but I wondered if he recognized the subtle changes that had taken place at home while he was away.

My independent, urban mother and I underwent major changes as we became more accustomed to the ways of Hiroshima. The Tamura family was also opening their eyes to our preferences. The women of the household, including Grandmother, began to try wearing simple one-piece casuals, without the layers required of kimono wear, during the humid summer months. The style was called *appappa*, describing its plain unpretentious appearance. They still preferred dressing up in kimonos, but these dresses were more practical and much cooler.

Another subtle change was in Aunt Fumiko, who rarely made any contrary remarks to any one. We noticed as she became more lively and talkative, even with her husband. Grandmother and Aunt Kiyoko were also more open to my mother's cooking Western cuisine. Mama was allowed on occasion to cook European and Chinese-style foods.

With close ties to her sister-in-law, and friends among the parents of my classmates, Mama was also quickly becoming more comfortable with being a Tamura. Our trips around the city were free of charge by using family passes we got because Grandfather was a major stockholder in the Hiroshima Dentetsu, the electric/utility, and the transportation company. Mama accumulated more kimonos, in modern fabrics chosen from the wide assortment of fabrics brought regularly to the Tamura estate by a sales representative. The kimonos for the Tamura women were ordered from home and then custom-made.

The clan members and their families congregated with each other frequently on one social occasion after another. Their grand homes would be open, as they served elegant festive food for the *oyobare* partying. The children played together like a big junior clan as well. The comforts of being a Tamura even with all its dues were finally becoming more apparent in all of our lives.

Papa also worked his way through the ranks, becoming an officer, and was allowed to commute from home. He coached Aunt Fumiko's younger brother on how to qualify for the officer candidates' corps, the *kanbu kohosei*. If one had no choice but to enter the military, this was the way to go without the formal schooling needed to become a career service man. Papa had passed the test at the time he was drafted, so he moved up fairly quickly. I, however, would not have wished to undergo the terrifying training that the grown men were being subjected to in the vast *renpei-jo*, the soldiers' training ground next to Seibi Academy. I saw both young and old soldiers being punched, shoved, and kicked. I wanted to cry and run as I passed by. Now and then the battering man in the uniform yelled at me for paying attention to the scene. I tried to walk looking only straight ahead, still failing to feel indifferent.

Once I spoke about these incidents to Papa who, by then, as an officer, was allowed to commute to his base. He was quiet and said very little against the men. But he said that the army life was not like what I had seen, and that it was like a family that took care of one another in other ways. He took me with him to his base for me to see the workings of military life. One section of the base was reserved entirely for the cavalry regiment. It had a distinct equine scent. Soldiers were tending to the beautiful animals with affection and care. There were even pig pens. This must have been for the army consumption. But the thought never occurred to me. It was the first time I ever saw a live pig. The men who worked under Papa were cheerful and in good spirits, unlike those whom I saw on the training ground. From time to time father brought home a live turtle or a stray kitten found by his men and given to him for his little daughter. I looked forward to my return visits to the base instead of dreading their harsh torments.

The caring quality I saw in my father towards his men was much like the ways of his own father. Grandfather's three thousand employees included handicapped men and women who were given tasks within their ability to perform. I remember Ben-san, who had a severe curvature of the spine, had light duties and used to help in our garden. No one at our door begging for charity was turned away without being given food or clothing.

These acts of kindness were usually not talked about, but just carried out. On one rare occasion there was a disgruntled employee with special demands. The man climbed to the top of the huge chimney, which was about sixty feet high, and the factory had to be shut down to prevent any harm to the man. Grandfather simply waited until the man gradually tired of sitting up on the chimney and came down. When I see his photograph today, I see the strength of character distinct in his warm expression. This man was a Tamura that anyone could be proud of.

A short time after his return from China, Papa was discharged from the Army altogether. We were free to return to Tokyo again. Mama was ecstatic. In the fall of 1941, the happy threesome of my parents and me settled into another little house in Tokyo. This time we situated ourselves closer to Mama's family in Kojimachi. With our boxes unpacked, and furniture in place, we returned to our urban element again.

4

The Encroaching War

News of the government's great plunge came just as we had begun to settle down and renew our ties in Tokyo. On December 8, 1941, I saw the members of Mama's family scurrying around, talking to each other with serious and worrisome expressions. It was a gray winter day, when the news of the declaration of the Greater East Asian War reached our family on December 8, 1941, in the sixteenth year of the Showa Emperor. I sensed that something terribly wrong was taking place, without understanding the somber content that had been expressed in whispers among my relatives when I came home.

"The war has started," my aunts and uncle said to each other with uneasy expressions.

"What are you talking about? What war?" I asked.

"Japan is fighting the Americans and the British. They are our enemies now, besides Chang Kai Shek in China." I thought about my young uncle and my aunts' photo collection of foreign movie stars.

"They are fighting us? Can't we see their movies anymore? I love Chaplin," I said in amazement and shock.

"Hush, don't say anything loud. What if someone heard us and thought that we were unpatriotic?"

"Can't we ask?"

"No, not out loud."

"Are we going to be alright, Auntie? Can we win?"

The adults looked at each other and told me not to worry, as the news of a naval victory had been broadcasted. I had the feeling that they didn't know what to make of it for sure. They gave short replies, and I listened to them, unable to understand.

This new sentiment was difficult for Mama. She had lived in Tokyo for all of her life. She had grown up wearing dresses rather than kimonos, eating ice cream and parfaits more often than rice cakes. Seeing foreign residents was a daily occurrence, as we lived near embassies.

Our country was at war with the United States of America and the United Kingdom. The imperial decree had been issued to support this fact. The Emperor's War Decree was read, and the attack on Pearl Harbor was reported. The significance of these events remained very vague in my mind. I knew that something very big happened, but more questions were raised frequently.

The reality of such news took time to sink in. Until then, the war was fought somewhere far away. It came to our doorstep soon after the Imperial Decree was released. The dreaded red paper came to Papa again, shortly after my seventh birthday in January, less than two months after Pearl Harbor had been bombed. I still remember the contrast between my happy birthday celebration with friends and the desolate feeling that we all carried, as all could be taken away again while we celebrated. Papa was to report back to the army base in Hiroshima immediately.

For my parents, who had just moved back to Tokyo after my father was discharged from his tour of duty in Northern China, it was an eerie forecast of tragedy. Within a month after our arrival, we headed back to Hiroshima. Receiving a call to serve the

Emperor was an unsurpassed honor, but it was bad timing for all of us. With the cloud of battle duty hanging over Papa, we settled back on Grandfather's Hiroshima estate.

We journeyed back to Hiroshima, knowing that this time it would be for good. I was re-enrolled in Seibi Academy, and rejoined with my old teacher and classmates who were happy to see me back. Transferring back to my old school in Hiroshima, the Seibi Military Academy, was like a homecoming. I saw familiar faces and uniforms in navy blue, with red stripes at the collar and cuffs. They still fit snug as if I had never left. I did have to get used to the "old style" bathrooms and the running around barefoot in the school yard during physical education classes. I had just left a school with modern sanitation, an outdoor swimming pool, and an indoor gym.

The Nagata-cho Grade School was a showcase of modern education with facilities that the Seibi children of Hiroshima would have envied. The area was close to the Diet building and the cabinet members' residences and other wealthy families, including the prime minister's family, the Tojyos. The latter's children were in school when I was.

Seibi Academy was like an austere military compound, with tall, green poplar trees along spacious school yards. The teachers were firm and demanding but revered by the students. My teacher, Miss Yamaoka, was a young woman, fresh out of school, with a gentle face. She was very patient with me as I readjusted to the Seibi curriculum. As a part of the Japanese military establishment, the students underwent strenuous physical training that no other schools required.

Inside the school gate was a stone structure like a mausoleum in which were the *goshinei,* the sacred pictures of the Emperor and the Empress. One was not permitted to walk past the *goshinei* without some expression of deepest respect and humility. We were taught to give the deepest and most reverent bow, the *saikeirei,* reserved only for the highest authority.

I remembered the days in the Nagata-cho School when open eyes were not allowed to view the persons of the imperial family. When the Emperor and the Empress passed our school, we marched down to the street to greet them. Our heads had to remain in the *saikeirei* position, so that the imperial couple did not see any of our faces, that was, save one. I just couldn't resist my curiosity, so I looked up and saw the very sweet face of our Empress. No one else saw her, since our eyes were supposed to be bowed down to the ground. I had been told that one could lose eyesight from it, but thank heavens, nothing happened.

The mythical origin of Japan was described by our teacher with perfection. We memorized the story with great relish. We recited the story of how the land of the Rising Sun was created by a pair of celestial Gods by stirring muddy water, and droplets turned into our islands. The celestial grandson was sent down to a point in Kyushu Island to reign over all of Japan. There was no doubt in my mind that I was quoting a creation of history just as it happened 2600 years before. We sang commemorative songs about the one hundred million proud Japanese dedicating themselves to their country.

We rehearsed the military code of honor and the marching routine daily. Respects for the war heroes and the dead war heroes were paid in every formal activity. On the eighth day of every month, the anniversary of the war declaration, the students marched to pay homage to the National Guardian, the Gokoku Shrine. The children whose fathers had died in action lined up in the front. The line was beginning to have more and more children.

Those who had sacrificed their lives in a very special way were called *gunshin*, military saints. We were taught that the seven men chosen to act as undersea human torpedoes in the attack on Pearl Harbor were seven *gunshins*. No one disputed their determination and courage, but I wondered why there were only seven, and not more. There were stories of each man going home to bid farewell to his family. They could not divulge the secret of their mission, but their mothers were proud to give their sons to their country.

We heard the praises of similar self-sacrifices in the war again and again, until it made us all feel that dying for our country was the most desirable fate. It gave us a sense of glory to die for a cause, the greatest of which was to die for the Emperor. I must confess, however, that I couldn't imagine myself becoming a human torpedo exploding underwater. On the other hand, I did envy boys who were heading for the special flying squadron forces, like the "Young Eagles" of the *Kasumigaura*. Soaring in the sky, as free as a bird, seemed so inviting. Becoming a Kamikaze pilot against an enemy denounced by all did not seem so horrible.

I also remember public references to Americans and British being "evil" or "subhuman." A newspaper showed a front page photograph of a young American girl smiling with a skull of a Japanese soldier on her desk. No Japanese person could possibly have pictured himself or herself doing the same thing with the skull of an American.

From time to time, flashbacks from my early childhood returned. I used to see blond and blue-eyed little girls or boys walking with their graceful mothers by our house near the foreign embassies in Tokyo. We used to wave and smile at each other. I couldn't imagine that they could possibly have anything to do with demons.

I also remember my own mother was accused of accepting the ways of the enemy because of her Occidental fashions. We were coming home from my school. It was a blustery winter day for which she dressed herself in an Astrakhan coat, with a matching hat and high heels. She was accosted by a man claiming to be a *kenpei*, military police officer, who accused her of being an enemy sympathizer. Their conversation ended when she informed him that her husband was an officer of the Imperial Army. The man didn't know how right he was. It was not the elegant European-styled clothes she wore, as she would have looked well in any clothes. It was her spirit that could not be bent. He could not have seen her bookcase with the glass sliding door. In it, I can still see the lettering on the covers: Hermann Hesse, Gide, Wordsworth, Tolstoy, Chekhov, Dostoevsky, Edgar Allan Poe, and even *Gone with the Wind*. How could a *kenpei* have suppressed them all?

The free spirit that I brought back from Tokyo was tucked away inside myself for the most part. I still loved all of my European and American storybooks. As I've said before, on rainy days and on days when our teacher was absent, my classmates often asked to have me tell the stories of kings and queens and knights from another world. I was only too happy to oblige, becoming the regular class story-teller.

Our school days usually began with an assembly. The principal, who stood on a wooden platform a few feet off the ground, issued words of instructions and announcements. This was followed by the morning calisthenics performed to the lively sound of music from the loudspeaker. As the war progressed, stamina-building became more important, as if our lives depended on stretching our physi-cal capabilities. The daily drill began to include running long dis-tances. Being able to carry a partner on our backs while marching was also included in the mandatory exercises. The only way one could be excused from these activities was to pass out from exhaus-tion.

During morning and lunch hours, there was additional stamina-building in which we stripped ourselves down to our underpants, in order to give our bodies a wet or dry washcloth rub for twenty to thirty minutes. In the dead of winter and in the scorching summer heat, we went on rubbing our bodies furiously, calling out numbers, "one, two, three . . ." The teachers praised us when our skin glowed pink, proof of a job well done. For older girls it was painfully embarrassing to stand unclothed before the boys of the same age and male teachers, but this was wartime.

The competitive sports activities were of no less importance. Passing performances in gymnastics, short and long distance run-ning, hurdles, jumps, vaulting, bars, rope climbing, and throwing were required. Failure was not acceptable. One worked until one performed adequately. The performances were closely timed, re-corded, and rewarded accordingly. The red badge was the highest merit, and blue and brown ranked below it. I wore the red with pleasure after I put in a laborious effort to achieve it, performing fifty front wheels on the bar and nearly killing myself from exhaustion.

Homework was compulsory during school holidays, over the new year, and throughout spring and summer. One of the require-ments was an illustrated diary. The great pain of not remembering daily activities, in addition to producing drawings to match them, were common headaches to most of us at the end of a long vacation. Still, there were always one or two children who had elaborate and exemplary journals which would be displayed for all to see with excerpts that were read to less ambitious children. I usually had to struggle even more in science. We had to return with an invention or a special collection of some sort every summer. The most popular collections were of insects and plants, and the most popular gadget was a sandwheel.

By the winter and spring of my fourth grade year, however, the mood of our country was changing drastically. The war losses were slowly coming to light. Battleships were lost in great numbers at Midway and Guadalcanal. My first real sense of grief came when the principal announced at our morning assembly that the troops stationed at Attu Island met the fateful *gyokusai* suicidal end. We sang for the fallen heroes.

> To the Sea
> A willing corpse in water.
> To the mountain
> A willing corpse in the thickets.
> Never turning back,
> As we serve our Supreme Master.

The melody was set to an ancient poem written by a centurion guard who was sent to defend the remote borders of our islands. We compared his patriotism of early ages to the reality of the war being fought in the South Seas.

After the Marshall Islands fell, B29's began to attack Northern Kyushu. Stories of the houses burned and the people killed began to reach everyday citizens. Goods were quickly disappearing from the market. Ration systems established earlier by the government for the necessities, such as food and fuels, were extended to clothing. By 1943, nineteen-year-olds were being taken to the war front. Stores closed without goods to sell. Factories shut down without fuel and manpower, except those that had converted to producing weapons. Grandfather stood his ground and insisted that his was a peacetime industry. The plants were barely able to operate with drastically reduced labor forces and depleting supplies.

Food was becoming scarce, but because of Papa's position as an administrator of military transportation for the Inland Sea bases, we had more food supplies than the average family. His men transported goods when supplies were needed. Still, there was not enough rice for three meals any longer. Grandmother and Aunt Kiyoko presided over dumpling soup for lunch and sometimes supper. What rice we did have had to be mixed with grains and soy beans—something which would have been unthinkable in peace-time. White rice was as dear as gold to everyone.

Being thrifty and resourceful, Mama had no trouble converting anything available for use. Our tablecloths and curtains turned up as casual wear for the family. She found ways to refine brown rice by putting it in an empty Sake bottle, and churning a wooden stick in it up and down. It was obviously a tedious process, but Mama seemed to relax with the motion. We would sit and talk as she tirelessly swished the rice up and down.

The school children still found time to do things they loved. We did school projects in each others' houses just as before. My best friend, Miyoshi, came to my house to complete an illustration of how charcoal is made. We used watercolors and chattered all afternoon, munching on goodies that Mama served. We marveled frequently at geniuses among us, such as Kimiko Nishimoto, who was not only outstanding in every subject, but also an accomplished musician. Her piano playing was so beautiful that even our music teacher lost track of the time. I had no idea at that time that these would be our last remaining years together.

The Tamura children attending the Seibi Academy walked to school together every day. The air raids were rampant, and the older children looked after the young. The older ones, Cousin Hideyuki and Cousin Kiyotsune, were beginning to notice pretty girls in school. I was starting to notice some of their athletic friends. I also admired Cousin Kiyotsune's gymnastic ability. Cousin Kiyotsune and I waited for one another to walk home together, chatting about this and that. Once he began asking me whom I really liked, calling out names and asking yes or no. He saved his name for last. How sweet he was. I never got to tell him that I admired him the most sincerely.

We still played and kept busy doing things. One night Cousin Hideyuki and I decided to hunt for bats near the house just before dark. We fought off the notion that stalking bats would bring misfortune. We went around hitting the poor creatures, one after another, and hung them on the pole before returning. The house was dark, and the family was frantically looking for us. Grandfather fell ill with a chest pain. We felt as though we caused his illness by our behavior.

During the ensuing weeks, he improved some, but in less than a month, just as he was recovering from pneumonia, he died from a heart attack caused by hardening of the arteries. He was sixty-two years old. My favorite gentleman and the revered patriarch was no more. Everyone was away at the time, with the exception of Auntie Kimie, who was with him when he died. It was an ironically fitting farewell, with only the daughter whom he seldom saw in private in attendance.

His body was draped in a white kimono and laid in the room of Buddha on a white silk futon, with his face covered by a soft cloth for the wake. The family sat in the room all through the night keeping vigil as his soul crossed the river of Sanzu, the three ways to Beyond. The mourners came from all around the country. Thousands paid respects to the businessman who led the industrial development of Hiroshima. The main gate was opened for the funeral procession and the hearse was driven over the marble driveway.

We took turns placing portions of his ashes in an urn after the cremation. I saw Papa weeping for the very first time. His military uniform did not stop him from expressing his grief. Picking up a piece from what may have been Grandfather's shoulder, Papa looked at it thoughtfully, and remembered how his shoulder had hurt so often. I was sobbing the whole time. So wept Auntie Kimie, though without sound and behind the crowd. A few months later, she disappeared from the house, in the middle of night, while everyone slept. My parents were suspected of having aided her departure, as Auntie Kimie's tiny room was just behind ours, and she could not have left without our knowledge. My parents denied any knowledge, but I know Mama heard from her unfortunate sister-in-law occasionally. Mama told me that Auntie Kimie was finally very happy. The year was 1943. This was the year of the beginning of the massive defeats of the Japanese military.

Uncle Hisao became the heir, in charge of running what was left of grandfather's company. He decided to run for city council, and won with a vigorous campaign. On the night of the victory, the grand *zashiki* remained lighted until dawn, and the night rang with the sound of celebration and the movement of arms raised in repeated *banzai's*. Papa, on the other hand, began to be more and more quiet as the days passed. He came home late, so I hardly saw him. His knowledge of the true predicament of the Japanese military was taking away his sleep and his peace of mind.

Sometimes I could not help but notice Papa's intoxication, requiring Mama's help to make it back to the room. All the ships he was sending out with supplies to the Pacific bases were being sunk. The Allied submarines had free reign of the Inland Sea, the very water of his homeland. Despite the turmoil, he still lent a hand with a last minute art project I had trouble with. He was pleased with my progress in my pencil sketches, and continued to guide me in the importance of light and perspective in my drawing.

Within a year, Mama's hometown, Tokyo, was incinerated by B29 Bombers. It crushed my mother to see a picture of Tokyo burning on the front page of the newspaper. She sobbed for a long time. Luckily, Grandmother Tome and my aunts and uncle were unharmed. Soon afterwards, they were evacuated to Okayama prefecture, Grandmother's hometown. We never heard from Auntie Kimie after the raid. She had been living in Tokyo. It was rumored that a search by her distant relative at the time had uncovered her charred body.

Bomb shelters were dug everywhere, and water was stored in hurriedly built cement cisterns near houses. Drills were repeated time and again on how to put out the fires caused by the incendiary bombs. B29's were now all over Hiroshima prefecture in air raids.

The first attack siren went off in the middle of the night. We ran to the shelter and stayed there all night. The raids were repeated night after night, until no one left the house any more.

By day, students were sent home when the warning sirens sounded. We were studying less and less. All of our clothes had labels sewn in with our names and addresses. Mama gave specific instructions for me to follow in time of the final assault on our land. Having survived the great Tokyo earthquake, she said the most important thing was to leave as quickly as possible, so that the fire would not surround you. She gave me step by step instructions to follow in the event of a direct hit in an air raid. She told me to hang on to solid furniture so that if the house was crushed, there might be space created at the bottom, and, further, told me to run towards the river as fast as possible, making sure to protect my head with a hood or cushion during the escape. Bombers often returned to kill off the fleeing. She repeated these instructions over and over until they were etched in my mind. I listened with a sense of disbelief, as I never realized that tomorrow might not be just like today.

Kamikaze missions were being flown and hailed. The fuel for the planes was running out. The draft age was lowered to seventeen, and even middle school children were mobilized to do public labor. In spite of this gloomy outlook, Cousins Hideyuki and Kiyotsune looked forward to attending the prestigious First Hiroshima Middle School after passing tough entrance examinations.

In 1945, school age children, in the sixth grade and under, were ordered out of cities in mass evacuations. Meetings were immediately convened for the parents of Seibi Academy students, and plans were formulated for a mass evacuation. The date of departure was set for April 10, 1945.

5

"So You May Be Saved, Children"

For weeks Mama worked at her sewing machine, whipping up my clothes, *zabuton* cushion, and futon. The list of supplies needed for my life in the country went on. There was a weight limit for how much could be allowed, so Mama kept on checking the bundle's weight, until the final packing, the day before. She was up most of that night fixing my *obento* lunch box for the train ride, carefully going over every item placed, and making sure it was labeled. Mama had to exhaust her rations and go far away to find the assortment of foods she packed for me. With the sinking of military supply ships, my father's source for goods was disappearing. In my lunch box I would find such hard to find items as eggs, fishcakes, sweet beans, Shiitake mushrooms, and even white rice all attractively packed.

We went over the contents of my bundle in detail. Mama had saved a little pouch for last, which she placed in my hand. "This is part of us," she said, "Papa's nail clippings and my hair." Mama said that this was a time of emergency, and we had to be prepared for anything to happen. In such a case, I would have something from them.

I was stunned. I had simply understood that we were going away because cities were being bombed and, it was dangerous for the children to stay in those areas. But I *hadn't* connected it to my parents actually being killed. It was unthinkable and unallowable. Sensing my grief, Mama reassured me that this was only in case of an extreme *if*, and that they would be waiting for me to come home when the war ended. I asked her how long she thought it might be. Mom's reply was hesitant. She didn't know. She added jokingly that if she could survive the Tokyo earthquake, she was going to be around for a long time.

The time for departure had finally come. On the morning of April 10, 1945, a sea of children and their parents, many weeping or fighting back their tears, assembled in the Hiroshima Station Square in the predawn hours. The parents were there to bid farewell to their sons and daughters who were being evacuated. Speeches were given, reassuring us that we must endure our hardships only until Victory, and that the children were to carry on as though the teachers were our parents now.

Headmasters of each school took roll calls and *Banzai* hails to the Emperor were belted out in unison before the march into the station began. I was a drill mistress for the girls' group from the Seibi Academy. I could not have maintained my composure without such tasks to perform. I did my best until I spotted Mama covering her face with a handkerchief in the dark. That ended all my composure. Tears that welled up in my eyes came streaming down. The station and the people became blurry, but I kept on marching, calling out the drill.

The loudspeaker was calling to instruct the parents not to enter the platforms or to come inside the station, so that the orderly procession of the children could continue without further delay or confusion. Respect for authority and order, however, was not to be shown that morning. There were parents everywhere waving good-byes and searching for their young ones for one last look. All the children realized, then, the real possibility of never seeing their parents again. We were being spared from the hideous pounding of the bombing.

The trains began to move, at last, towards their many distant destinations, with choking smoke, shushing sounds, and crying children aboard. We were leaving behind waving adults swarming over the train tracks. At the first crossing there were more adults. Hiroshima was bidding a farewell to its young children.

We were dazed with puffy eyes, but we still looked out to the passing panoramic mountain ranges, towns, villages, and rice fields. We ate our delicious *obentos* and munched on leftovers. It was much like a school outing before the war, when food was abundant, and the kids looked for adventures. The energy associated with these past events was lacking, however. I was tired as I looked over to the younger girls in my group who were still crying after hours had passed. I felt duty bound somehow to comfort them, without knowing what I could possibly say to them. I had no idea what life in Kimita Village might be like. We were exhausted from the impact of the day's events as we rode farther and farther from Hiroshima.

"Miyoshi, Miyoshi," the station master's voice uttered through the loudspeaker, as the Seibi teachers hurried their students off the train, at the end of nearly an all day train ride. "This is where we get on buses that will take us to our villages," the head teacher called out. We followed him to the spot where our buses were waiting.

The unfinished leg of our journey began as we boarded a caravan of buses in Miyoshi and then drove along winding mountain passes for hours, while twilight was setting in over the mountain ranges and thatched-roofed houses. The dimming view gave way to a darkness as the caravan huffed and puffed its way up the last stretch over a steep mountain pass. It was pitch dark when we were awakened by a shrill voice, announcing that we had finally arrived at the foot of our destination, Zensho Temple.

The vehicle was too large to travel on the tiny path to the temple, so the children walked slowly to the bottom of the stone steps and climbed forty-some steps to the gate at the top, where the people of Kimita village had prepared a welcome banquet for us.

It had been an exhausting journey. All we cared about at that point was rest. When we were led to rows of tables with the best possible country spread, we simply stared at it. The farmers who knew about the food shortage in the cities had thought that the little children would devour the good food. But on this day, all of our parents had worked miracles, gathering special treats like it was our last meal, and we had eaten more than enough for the day already. The teachers realized the delicate situation, and nudged us to eat and clean up our plates as a show of gratitude. It could not be done. We were too tired to eat and too full. A group of forty some children, numb and frightened, sat in silence, motionless.

When I saw the smiling faces of the women stiffening, I sensed the awkward situation. I feebly attempted to thank them for the banquet and tell them that we were really very tired since it had been a very long day. It did not change the villagers' obvious disappointment.

Chaos followed after our unhappy hosts left us, and the tables were cleared away. We dashed for our futons and bundles to save a spot next to our friends so we could sleep beside each other for the night. No one, including the teachers, knew which directions the futons should be laid in, or how many rows. In the end we simply did as we saw fit, since, for the first time, there were no strict orders to obey.

Miyoshi and I sent eye signals to each other to save a place for the other, and soon, the rest of the girls had managed to put their futons together. As soon as the talking subsided, the sound of sobbing started here and there. I saw Miyoshi pulling her covers over her face, but before her face disappeared, I saw her red eyes. "I don't want to cry. No, I'm not going to cry." I fell asleep my first night away from home saying these words.

The morning came, sooner than anyone had expected, with more surprises. The wake up call from the teachers brought us back to the reality of our new temple home. There was no running water for wash-ups for us. We were told to go down the steps to a small stream at the foot of the hill. Having had no prior experience in outdoor camping, we were lost. "There's a first time for everything. Let's make an adventure out of this," I said to Miyoshi. We ran down the steps to the water. Frogs were jumping and the minnows were swishing by as we tried to scoop up enough water to wash our faces. It was very cold. The air was chilly, even for April. By the time we finished, we were shivering from head to toe.

A morning sutra, a chanting of verses from the holy texts, was the next order before the breakfast, led by a priestess whose husband had been taken to the battle front. A pretty red-cheeked young woman with a religious robe, and powerful voice, was in charge. Each morning, before sunrise, the service began with resounding gongs. We sat on our knees, shivering in the chapel and clutching the sutra texts in our hands, belting out *namuamidabutsu* along with the priestess. We had very little idea about what we were chanting except that our breakfast came after this.

Sometimes the sutra chanting felt as if it were endless, and at other times, it seemed short. The time passed quickly after we memorized the lines, and in a relatively short time, we all knew our lines rather well. When the chanting finally concluded, we rushed to line up with our rice bowls for breakfast. The long rows of narrow tables were laid out on the open corridor of the chapel, exposed to the elements. Sitting down on the cold floor, with knees properly tucked under, was uncomfortable, but it was compulsory, except for those excused for a physical disability.

After our hurried breakfast came our first trip to the village school, at the top of a small mountain. We had to climb over two hundred steps to get to the top. We were continually aware of the curious stares from the villagers along the way. By the time we had climbed half of the stone steps to school, we were ready to go home, as we could not imagine how we were going to make it to the top every day. We wondered how anyone could have decided to put a school on a mountain top.

The sight of a few village children walking down the steps with cleaning rags and buckets scared us to death, as we believed that the crew was descending for water, which we would have to carry back up again. It turned out to be a false alarm, as we saw an outdoor pool on the school playground that was filled with muddy water which was used for washing and cleaning.

The Kimita elementary school was a spacious, two-story building. There wasn't much playground equipment. We didn't see any factory-built jungle gyms, but did see a large wooden jungle gym, held together by ropes through which the children climbed and moved about. It seemed to be quite popular, so that I even tried it for a bit and found it to be fun. Steel bars caught my eyes. I wanted to try them right away, but was too out of breath after the long climb to do anything more. We stood around feeling and looking more lost than on the previous day, as the village children looked on with questioning stares.

Luckily, our identities were preserved in the classrooms. The Seibi Academy children formed their own groups. In Seibi sixth grade classes, boys and girls were put together while the teachers were shared. The class arrangement became quite inconsequential, for in the end, we attended school only on rainy days and worked outdoors for the rest of the time. We hadn't known that this would happen when we left home.

The kind of work to which we were assigned was beyond our physical capabilities and life experiences. We were required to dig up giant pine roots and build hearths from scratch in order to extract pine oil for airplane fuel. One group of children took the shovels, and the other group carried backgear used for transporting heavy rocks. My shoulders became raw in no time at all, rubbing against the straps which were weighed down by the heavy rocks. I requested a change of work to digging, but it turned out to be no easier.

We were also sent out onto the mountainside in small groups to collect edible plants as the food sources were becoming scarce. The villagers were unable to keep us supplied. We learned quickly which grasses were edible and tasty, and which side of the mountain had more curly fern buds. One had to be careful not to get lost on the mountain, however. More than a few children strayed from the group and got lost, including myself. There was an eerie feeling being lost in the thicket and tall trees. It was both scary and tranquil. I kept myself from being tempted to go back again.

Bathing arrangements for the forty children initially took a little time to work out. For a while, at the end of a heavy, perspiring work day, we had to go to bed without a good washing. In no time at all, we found lice in our hair, for the first time in our lives. The girls, who had never even heard of such things, cried their hearts out. They felt shabby and ashamed. At first there were whispers about who had head lice, but pretty soon everyone had them. No cures or rinses were provided. We behaved like a tribe of grooming monkeys, bending over a friend's head picking lice eggs out of her hair, and she returned the favor. The incessant itching drove us to constant irritation and discomfort.

Eventually our group was divided into groups of three and four that would go to neighboring farmhouses for bathing, once or twice a week, in return for drawing all the bath water and building the fires to heat the water.

Most farmhouses had no wells with pumps. The water had to be drawn by hand. We took turns dividing the chores. The hardest task by far was filling up the deep iron tub with buckets carried from outside. Still, we loved our bathing day, sitting down with friends, checking on the fire, and talking idly while we waited for the nice warm bath. For a very short time, it felt like we were back home again.

Learning the ropes in the country was bittersweet. Soon after my first try at the bar, which was my favorite exercise during break periods in the school yard, the village children, mostly boys, began to taunt me everywhere I went. They were chanting my name and chanting an address where their desired encounters could take place. The expressions made little sense to me at the time. I thought it would just go away. It didn't. In the school yard, in the field, during pine root digging, and elsewhere, the taunting became a persistent attention getter, and an ordeal for me. I tried to ignore it, but the taunting continued. I told them I didn't understand their actions and asked them to stop. They just looked at each other and giggled. I realized that the content of the teasing had had to do with a forbidden or embarrassing subject. I pretended they weren't there, but the loud and haunting calling voices never ceased.

I was pleasantly surprised one morning during this period. I ran into a sympathetic village youngster. I was collecting edible grasses on a rice field patch, and something moved under my foot. It was a black snake. I gave a loud scream and jumped away, totally shaken. A friendly voice and a reassuring face popped into my vision. He told me it was a harmless snake and I didn't have to be afraid.

I hadn't noticed him standing there before. He came out of nowhere. Unlike other children, his face was fair, without a dark tan, just like city children. He was the first village boy who didn't taunt me. I was relieved. We encountered each other often after that day. His name was Takada, a young son from a large farm house, down the road where the bus had brought us earlier. Takada was always wearing a red cap, so I could spot him far away. We exchanged books and thought well of each other.

Back at the temple, daily conversation among the girls concerned food and hunger. "I'm so hungry" became our common greeting. If anyone's parents sent her any food, it was to be shared by everyone. But it was not possible for any of the parents to send so large a quantity, so children usually kept the food to themselves, using it also for an exchange of favors. Some favors were exchanged between a teacher and favored children. Ms. Kamio, a widowed teacher for our group, was said to be dispensing special treats to children who were fragile. It was usually kept a secret. Just who might have been fragile was questionable. All of us had to have passed the physicals to be there. I could not believe it when my turn for such special treatment came up. I was served a bowl of sweet cornstarch treat with a stern warning not to tell anyone about it. Gifts to the teacher, I learned later, was the key.

Ms. Kamio was paired with a married male teacher, Mr. Masaki, whose wife remained in the city. They had separate rooms in the family quarters, on the back side of the temple. Mr. Masaki was very shy with our parents, but he was quite talkative with the girls. He used to unroll the girdle over his khaki pants, complaining about his swollen calves, and pinching to show us how far his fingers sank into his fair-skinned flesh. We really couldn't see the difference as we pinched our own in comparison. He was very stern with any infractions, however.

At one point, I made it to a dentist for cavity work. I rode with

Miyoshi's mother who was visiting. I assumed mistakenly that I had had the teacher's permission to go. Mama had worked out an arrangement with the dentist and Mr. Masaki. It was apparently not to his satisfaction. Public reprimand went on for an extended period when I returned. Ms. Kamio joined Mr. Masaki saying that I had been overzealous in my leadership over our study group to which her own daughter belonged. I had suggested to my study group that we might try to become a role model for the rest of the girls, by working harder than we had back home. To me it was one way to fulfill the wishes of our parents who always got after us about studying. I had thought that our parents would have wanted us to give our best effort. Ms. Kamio felt it was not necessary. She complained that my suggestion of being a role model embarrassed her daughter. Being chewed out in front of the entire group by the two teachers, in spite of my best effort to please them, left me with a feeling of despair. I sat and cried inconsolably. I told Miyoshi I did not think I could bear these circumstances much longer. She agreed.

Our letters home were censored by the teachers, who refused to mail any correspondence that even hinted that we were unhappy. My first letter was rejected, and only the most flowery comments went through thereafter. There were a few children who managed to send for their parents to come get them. The first student who went home with her mother, after barely a month in the country, claimed her delicate health as the reason. The girls lined up waving their good-byes. We all wished our health would fail so our parents might do the same for us.

There were plenty of health-related problems. The biggest headache for the teachers was the problem of bedwetting. Each morning someone woke up crying from having wet her futon. Miyoshi and I almost got into a fight one morning when I woke up in a drenched futon after she had slept in my bedroll with me. My underwear was completely dry but hers wasn't. I had to keep her out of my futon after this incident.

Some girls developed chronic enuresis. It was frightening and embarrassing to lose bladder control during the night, but even more terrifying to watch the consequences. The chronic wetters were taken to a village acupuncturist, who also administered *okyu*, skin burning with dried moss placed on certain parts of one's body. I was taken with the girls who wet their beds. Previously, on damp days, I had had pain in my knee joints and the pain recurred. The teachers felt that *okyu* on my knees might be beneficial, but changed their minds and decided to use acupuncture after my vehement protests that my parents would not allow any scarring of my knees.

I nearly fainted, however, when the "healer" took out the long thin needles from his black case. They looked like they were long enough to easily go straight through my small knees, or any other part of my body. He saw my obvious terror and reassured me that it would not hurt. I didn't believe him. When my turn came I held my breath and body as tight as I could, preparing for the worst sting and pain I could imagine. It was not necessary. I felt like a hero watching the long thin needle disappear into my skin while I didn't even have to flinch.

One night a week we were given these acupuncture and *okyu* treatments and I watched the girls wailing and begging to be excused. The girls sat neatly on *tatami* mats while the moss pieces were heated up on their backs. The method was meant to be a cure for the bedwetting, though I can't recall a single time it worked.

One afternoon, I decided to send my parents a real letter without censorship, and posted the card myself on my way back to the temple, when I passed the village post office. The reaction was swift. Homemade cookies and more parents began arriving at the temple to visit the children. From the elevated temple grounds, we craned our necks to look for anyone getting off at the bus stop in the middle of the day.

I learned, then, Mama had just lost a baby after seven months of pregnancy. I had had no idea that she was pregnant while she was making the long trips to the temple by riding trains and shaky buses. This probably did not help Mama, who had had other miscarriages before. I contracted a full-blown case of measles. A caretaker was needed and mother's help was sought. Because

Mama was convalescing herself, she sent her own health aide to my side. As soon as my fever went down, I managed to knit a pair of booties for my deceased baby sister, Toshiko, named after our maternal grandfather, Toshi. I sent a note asking my parents to place the booties at her altar.

Miyoshi and I remained convinced that our lives were more endangered staying at the temple, being lice-infested and hungry, and receiving a minimal education. I was also developing chronic stomach problems, and was unable to chew due to frequent toothaches. I told Mama that I would not dare return to the dentist because of the trouble it had caused before. We wrote in more detail of our plight, until finally, both sets of parents consented to come get us. There could not have been a happier pair of children. The group had already thinned out, for many had already gone home or to other relatives in the country. We were the envy of the remaining children.

On the afternoon of August 4, 1945, Miyoshi's mother and mine climbed the long steps of Zensho-Ji to come for us. We ran out and hugged our mothers, the liberators of our detention work school. Miyoshi and I were like a pair of two little kittens, snuggling up to our liberators. The two mothers suggested that they might stay an extra day to rest up before going home. We were so eager to leave, however, that we protested. We begged not to be forced to stay another extra moment there. We desperately wanted to go home. The mothers would have stayed if we hadn't protested so hard. It would have been so easy to have stayed out of the catastrophe that was to come.

At dawn we left Kimita Village on a horse cart, for there was no bus at so early an hour. We boarded a truck from a town where one of the Tamura clan had evacuated his plant and had a regular trucking route back to Hiroshima. We arrived home by late afternoon, tired and sore after a long ride. Cousin Hideyuki and I played just like old times when he returned from his middle school. We talked and talked. I asked him about the meaning of the village boys' taunts, but he couldn't figure them out either. We expected our endless childhood to go on as before.

His school was meeting in shifts and was sending him out to the center of the town the next day to assist with clearing the torn down buildings. The city was clearing debris so that the fires from the incendiary bombings could be better contained. Mama was also preparing a lunch for a similar assignment the next day. I did not understand why others in the household could not be made to go. I wanted so much to have more time with her. She thought I was taking it all too seriously, as she said that we had all the time in the world to be together after she returned for lunch time. We slept soundly at the end of a long journey home.

6

The Death of Hiroshima

The morning after our return from Kimita Village was quite remarkable. I could hardly believe I was waking up to the sounds of a summer morning at home. A tranquil stretch in the privacy of my own room was a luxury I had forgotten in the country. A new sense of gratitude welled up in my body, as I thought about the hardships left behind. No more mad dashes to the cold stream for wash-ups at dawn. No more heavy rocks to carry on my back, or going to bed with muffled sounds of weeping in the darkened room after the lights were out. The list was endless. There was a tinge of guilt from thinking about my homesick and hungry classmates but only for a few moments. I had no regrets about hurrying back home.

The sun was shining in the garden. For now, I was returning to being a child again, with the protective arms of my parents around me, without the harsh regimen of yesterday. A breakfast of rice porridge was on a tray with a soft, pickled sour plum, so I didn't have to chew. My toothache still persisted.

Mama was trying to decide whether or not to go to her mandatory community task of tearing down the empty houses in town. Left vacant after the government ordered the evacuation, the houses were ready to be burnt down in the event of any incendiary bomb attacks. This was one of the things she could have avoided, had we stayed back one more day, but Miyoshi and I had protested so adamantly that the mothers relented, and came back a day earlier.

She was debating until the last moment whether to stay home in order to spend more time with her daughter on her first day home. I watched Mama as she packed a few sweet dumplings for snacks, and heard her say she made them for her daughter. Mama asked me if it was all right to take some for herself. Of course it was, I replied. Mama said she would try to be let out early or slip away by lunch break, anyway. I walked Mama to the back entrance door, seeing her off with a smile, but grumbling inside about her "obligation" to leave me so soon. Mama waved a quick good-bye. "See you just in a short time." The words faded away as she hurried off.

A paperback story about a Samurai duel from my cousin, Hideyuki, was at my side. He had left it for me to read the night before, when I asked him for something amusing. I laid back on the futon, feeling a little bit weak from a lack of solid food.

A typical summer day was about to begin with a gentle breeze on my face and bare back, and I wore just my underpants. I was very relaxed when the air raid warning siren went off around 7:15 A.M. or thereabouts. It was a familiar sound by then, but I turned on a radio to find out what it could be all about anyway. A casual warning was being issued, stating three enemy planes were en route towards our city. "Only three?" I shrugged. It was hardly worth being warned about. Hundreds maybe, but three?

I remembered the first time they came in the middle of night. The sounds of hundreds of flying planes in the dark night sky had paralyzed me with fear. I remembered clutching Mama and asking her, "Mama, are we going to be hit? Are we going to die?" She was very quiet. She told me that she didn't know, but we were together, whatever should happen. Somehow, being with my mother and hearing her words gave me a small respite, even under the deafening sounds of death looming so closely.

All of the drills we had practiced: running to the bomb shelter, exercising rescues, and putting out fires, were not used. There were air raids and bombings all of the time while I was away, but our neighborhood had not been targeted, at least it seemed. I felt safe.

I also thought about Cousin Hideyuki's obsession with the B29's that filled the sky in the past. He slipped out of our concrete bomb shelter, tucked deep in the garden, behind the trees and the rocks. Before anyone noticed, he was on the rooftop with a pair of binoculars. He was trying to get a closer look at the shape and design of the flying enemy. His mother and the rest of the family would be frantic about his safety, screaming for him to come back down. His fascination with what he considered superb mechanical objects did not wane with any amount of chastising.

I kept the radio on to hear the conclusion of the warning, even though an air attack by three planes seemed less than alarming. A simple announcement came on a little later around 7:30 A.M., that the planes had turned around. The warning signal was cancelled, indicating to people it was entirely safe for them to return to work outside. I went out in the corridor briefly and yelled, "The warning is off, everybody, the warning is off." I heard Aunt Fumiko replying from a distance, "We didn't pay much attention, Hideko, it's so nice out." Feeling every bit safe and sound myself, I turned off the radio and went back to reading my Samurai story. An intense duel between rival swordsmen was about to take place in the book. I was completely absorbed in the story looking down towards the printed pages, away from the open window to the garden.

Suddenly, without any warning, an immensely blinding flash crossed my eyes, riveting my attention. Instantly, I saw a huge band of white light plummeting past the trees and the stone lanterns to the ground, with a swift swishing sound like a massive gushing waterfall. There was nothing in my memory that corresponded with the terrifying image.

Almost simultaneously, a thunderous, deafening explosion jolted the air with an immediate violent quake, shaking the very foundation of the earth and everything that stood on it. The end of the world must have come, I thought to myself as I instinctively jumped to my feet with the memory of Mama's voice echoing in my head, "Find something strong to hold onto."

I tried to brace myself between a large vertical beam and a sturdy cupboard, but it was impossible to remain vertical or keep a steady grip as the entire structure was being jolted in so many directions. The space around me shrank with the frenzy of flying and breaking objects, falling on my head and naked body. It was dark all around me, as if the sun itself had disappeared, and the exploding earth raged in the thick black air and swirling wind. I could no longer see, but just felt the motion and the terror. So this is dying in the war. I didn't know how it would happen or what would happen next, but I expected to be broken in pieces and blown up in bits along with my house. My terror was combined with a strange feeling of being resigned to let it end without protest. Mama had always taught me to *live*. There seemed to be no other alternative but death, as the exploding earth continued to rage. I felt and remained powerless, while the endless motion persisted.

Suddenly, just as unexpectedly as it had begun, the wind and the motion stopped. It became completely still. The thick, dusty air began to clear. I found myself covered with soot and debris, but *alive*. The vertical beams I had sought to grab had held in spite of the long and vicious pounding, creating a small breathing space, so that I was protected from being crushed. I moved my body, pushing away broken objects around me. Out of a small open space, I could see the sun showering its soft rays over the green leaves and moss covered rocks. The unchanged sight was contradicting my assumption that one of the three planes sneaked back and dropped a bomb directly on our garden, which did not bear obvious signs of change like a bomb crater.

But just then, the memory of Mama's voice returned, "Hideko-chan, leave immediately before the fires surround you." Mom had taught me the dangers of fire in bombing attacks. She had told me about the people who couldn't get away, even after they survived the bombing itself. They were incinerated. A new surge of terror like a sharp pain ran through my body as I realized I was far from being safe, still trapped in the debris. I tried to clear a larger space so I could actually get out from under the house. The tangled pieces of broken objects were more difficult to push away than they appeared. I was frantic. Mama had not prepared me for this.

Out of desperation I yelled out a loud, "Help me someone, please help me." To my relief, Aunt Fumiko heard the cry and her faint voice traveled back. "Where are you, Hideko?" She guided me to a space where I could slowly make my way out. She was pretty banged up herself, but her baby daughter Kumiko had not received a scratch. Aunt Fumiko had held her body over her daughter like a shield, she said.

"What about Grandma Tamano and Auntie Kiyoko?" Aunt Fumiko and I called out their names. After several loud yells, the two women emerged, covered with torn clothing and cuts and bruises. Grandma Tamano had bruises on her head and was bleeding. Her oldest daughter, Kiyoko, was hurt in the back and shoulder. They were both in great pain and shock, moving about aimlessly. Suddenly, a voice of distinct agony came, resounding from the direction of the rear entrance. It was Fumiko's husband, Hisao, calling for help and looking for the family.

"I'm back, . . . Where are you, . . . Isn't anyone alive?" Aunt Fumiko hurried towards the fading voice, taking Kumiko. Fumiko's shrieking cry cut through the air shortly, "Oh, my God, oh no!" Uncle Hisao was sitting on the stone floor just inside the rear gate. His torn and blackened white shirt was stained in blood, and his hollow eyes stared out, while blood was streaming down from a gaping hole in the middle of his throat. His large body was covered by countless pieces of broken glass stuck into his skin.

Uncle Hisao had just made it out from under his collapsed plant. He was sitting at his desk going over the morning details, when the entire office building and the factory came crashing down to the ground. His large body took the breaking glass in full force, and a nail got stuck in his throat during the breaking frenzy of the explosion. He made it out miraculously, and hobbled back to his house, thinking that only the plant was hit by a bomb. He was groaning, "The end has come."

My uncle was sitting dazed and speechless, with eyes wide open, repeating over and over, *"Mo dame da*, This is the end, we are finished, this is the end." Aunt Fumiko was sobbing with her bruised limbs and her torn kimono. She was trying to cover his bleeding throat and to pick out the pieces of glass stuck in his skin.

I found myself covered with soot and bruises all over my body, but considering that I was mostly naked and unprotected, I was relatively unscathed save for a gushing cut from large broken pieces of glass in the sole of my right foot. The sight of blood was scary. Never having tended to my own cuts and bruises before, I was lost and helpless, despite the countless first aid drills in school. Chills went down my spine upon seeing shards of glass stuck in my foot.

Aunt Kiyoko and Grandma were in no shape to aid anyone else. I called for Aunt Fumiko's help again, showing her my predicament, but she was so occupied by her husband's dire state that she hardly took a look, saying she was sorry but she could not help me. Hisao needed her attention right away. I understood, then, there was no one but myself to look after my cuts. It was my very first taste of being alone with my own wounds; taking care of myself began for me on that day.

I hopped over to a pump well at the far end of the house and washed my hands and feet, before attempting to pick out the broken shards of glass stuck in my right foot. I flinched as I took out the pieces, to my surprise, with minimal pain. I found a pair of gym shoes and a few pieces of soft tissue, which I placed on my wound and put the shoes on my feet. I also found a pair of *mompe* slacks, my mother's long sleeve shirt jacket with her initials, K.T., on the chest pocket, a hood, and a cushion to protect my head, remembering her instructions, "Cover yourself as you escape, in case the air attack resumes."

Most important, Mama had said, after any bomb explosion, should you survive it, is to "leave as quickly as possible to get away from the danger of being trapped by fire." The point was illustrated time and again in the massive incendiary bomb attacks over Tokyo and other major cities. People were incinerated because they were trapped in an encroaching fire, designed to kill a maximum number of civilians. The bombers shot those that escaped, we were told.

I realized they could lose no time. I walked over to my relatives, urging them to flee, saying that there was no time to spare or they could lose their escape routes. The dazed adults who sat and lay under the shady tree in the garden did not so much as turn towards me. With blank expressions, they continued to nurse their wounds. I repeated my plea even louder, but there was no reply, as if they hadn't heard me at all. I wanted to cry. My Mama forbade waiting around if there was time to run. But there they were, sitting and waiting, for how long, I did not know. Oblivious to my terror, their refuge for now was in the comfort and safety of the still shady and peaceful garden, where they remained dazed and confused.

Just then, what I feared most happened. A huge ball of fire jumped into my vision, rising out of a medium-sized factory across the street. In a matter of seconds the fire grew into an engulfing orange-colored wave moving horizontally, and I knew that a shift in the wind could change its direction at any moment. I screamed in terror, shouting to my aunts and uncle several times, "Fire, fire, you've got to leave. You've got to get away!" No one responded. I could not wait. I yelled that I was leaving. Running down the steps to the street level, I kept on shouting, "Please leave!"

It was Mama's teaching which guided me then. I did exactly what Mama taught me to do in time of a dire emergency, step by step, as I was instructed before. I remembered all the steps.

I had no idea what awaited me outside of our house, which was shielded by the vast garden. I had assumed that a powerful bomb had hit our estate directly, or possibly, our factory was also hit simultaneously, because I had heard only a single explosion. But the entire neighborhood had changed its appearance. The buildings had collapsed all around, and there were people covered in torn clothing and blood just like Uncle Hisao.

I now understood more fully my uncle's words, the world *was* coming to an end. My first sight of injured strangers was of two women crawling on the ground near the main entrance gate. The young woman wore a bright colored top and a long skirt. The older woman had bloodstained white garb. They appeared to be Koreans. As soon as their eyes met my startled gaze, the younger woman

raised her hand towards me calling out in words I did not understand, while the older one remained silent, looking at me with
pleading eyes. They were asking me to do something, but what I
couldn't understand.

I stopped running momentarily, and tried to make out what they
were trying to say to me. Neither of the women tried to or could
speak in my language. I repeated in Japanese that someone might
come along who could help, but I couldn't. I was very sorry. In
another time, I might have run back inside to get help for them, but
the people inside the gate were no more able than those two
women.

The willingness to help strangers was a never talked about but
common practice in my household. My late grandfather led the way.
He hired disabled persons, who would not have had any job, when
others shunned them. Food was scarce, and meat was nonexistent
for most people, at that time. But when my grandfather, a devout
Buddhist, found out that a foreign Catholic priest was suffering a
long illness, he sent a package of beef with a note explaining that he
understood that foreign persons required meat in their diet, and he
hoped that this nourishment would help the priest back to health.

Walking away, I passed neighbors, disheveled and dazed, coming
out of their houses and leaving. They paid little attention to passers-
by. No one recognized me. It was as though I were invisible. Their
attention was fixed on getting out and looking for their own
families, an already overwhelming task.

The houses were caved in, crooked, and barely standing. Small
flames were starting to spread like torches, and the wind fanned
them swiftly into larger fire balls, terrorizing the fleeing people. I
thought I heard cries of people asking for help—perhaps help
pulling someone out of a crumbled house, someone who was still
trapped. But there was no more time nor power in my body except
to listen to Mama's voice. "Go to the water, child, stay close to the
river, save yourself from fire." With heart racing, I headed towards
the Ota River, limping and dragging my right foot. Soon, more
injured people were moving together in a silent march in the
general direction of the outer limits of the city.

Their bloodstained clothes were torn or singed black. Some were even bare. I did not know where all of these people were coming from. I tried to look for people I recognized so I could flee with them. There were no familiar faces. In the moving sea of horribly hurt people, no one seemed to notice a frightened, lost child. The once familiar call of *Ojo-san*, greeting me, never came. I was truly alone.

As I neared the Ota River, I saw a small group of adults and children, standing on the river bank with their hands clasped in prayer. An older man, like the head of a family, was directing them to pray for the safety of others left behind. Huge explosive sounds went off across the river every half minute in the background. There were no bombers in the sky, but the explosions continued from the direction of the army base. "They got the arsenals," someone said in horror.

I turned my face towards the center of the city, from which bellowing smoke rose. I closed my eyes, praying for the safety of my family, especially my parents, "Please God, please keep them safe." I had no idea where they could be. Papa was a transportation officer by the harbor, and Mama was with the mobilization force somewhere in the heart of town. As I prayed, my cheeks were wet from tears, for the first time. I repeated as if to be consoling myself, "Mama, I'm doing just exactly what you told me to do, now, please be safe."

Torn by worry over my parents, I could not help but wonder about the three planes that came and went, and the single explosion I heard. There must have been a huge direct hit, but how could it be that there was only one explosion? I did not understand, but the question was irrelevant. The task at hand was to escape and preserve my life.

The people moving toward the river began to merge from all directions. More and more of the injured flowed in. Suddenly, someone called my name. It was Noriko, a next door neighbor's daughter. Her face and arms were very red. She had just made it out of the schoolyard of her elementary school, and was escaping with her family.

"Nori-chan what happened to you?"

"There was this flash, and it burned me," Noriko said.

"Yes, I saw the flash, it was like a white waterfall. Did your school get a direct hit?" I asked.

"It must have," she guessed.

Noriko's skin was very red when I first saw her. Then, it turned into large blisters covering her forehead and one eye. Noriko's face became so swollen I could hardly recognize it anymore. She said some of the children were in much worse shape than she was. The children were too young to look after themselves like she did, and the injured teachers couldn't take care of them, either. She didn't know what happened to them. I was still very grateful that there was a family I could walk with, even though Noriko was in a great deal of pain and had stopped talking.

Along the river, we saw a young school girl slowly walking, with pieces of skin hanging from her arms. Someone said that she was trying to cool her burned skin, but as she rubbed the water on, her skin came off. She was crying out in pain. A Catholic sister who ran a nursery school in the same area told me that some of the small children had been so burned that it was difficult to tell which side of their faces were which. She said that the way she could tell, finally, was to look down to their shoes and see which direction the shoes were pointing in. The little children were crying and wandering around. We could not stop. We moved on like a herd with a will of its own.

The cuts on my foot started to bleed as I kept walking. I tried to rinse the wounds with river water, and then I tied a piece of cloth around my foot. Once or twice someone yelled, "An enemy plane is coming back!" We ran down to the river bed, wading in the water, and tried to hide under tall water weeds. I covered my head with the cushion Mama told me to carry.

"The assigned village for our refuge is 'Tomo Village,' " Mama's voice was returning again. I kept on walking, wondering where Tomo was. After a while, there were no more cries of a plane coming. It was a relief, as I was almost out of strength. I could not have run down to the water one more time.

I saw a large truck pulling up a few blocks away. It was picking up people from the roadside. The driver hollered and waved his hand, as he yelled, "Hurry, hurry, if you want a ride!" Noriko and her family made a dash, telling me to do the same. I didn't think I had any more strength left to push on, but made a last effort, hobbling towards the vehicle, as though it was my last chance to live. The truck was already full when I got there. I begged the driver for one more space, pointing to my injured foot, pleading that I just couldn't take another step. He shrugged and lifted me onto the already packed truck.

On the truck, I found myself the only fully clothed rider with a clean appearance as well as the only one without obvious bruises and cuts. We sat in silence while the truck bed rattled and shook with the rough country ride, until a woman, holding a small still child, began to talk. She looked around, speaking in a loud voice repeating where and what happened to her and her child. One or two people around her spoke briefly and then were silent again.

The truckload of people was let out in front of a small country hospital after about thirty minutes. The courtyard was jammed with hundreds of people standing and sitting on the ground, waiting to be treated, with more arriving all the time. Only the most injured, mostly burn victims, however, were being given any attention. Noriko received a coat of white cream on her face and arm only after waiting a long time and her parents' cutting in line and storming in, asking the medical staff to give her some attention. Noriko and her parents left after that, hoping to stay with a distant relative in the nearby countryside. There was no room left to stay where I was, but I had no idea in which direction I should travel or how far.

A young male villager was directing the traffic of people, dispensing a few grains of dried soy beans to the crowd, and urging them to move anywhere they might know someone, because they couldn't stay there. There was no other food, so I clutched the beans in one hand. I asked him if I could have my foot bandaged. He looked at me in amazement that such a minor hurt should be taking up anyone's time. I asked him if he knew where Tomo Village was.

He said he did, but had no time to explain, suggesting that I knock on some houses down the street.

I walked down the road and knocked on the door of a small house. I asked if anyone knew where Tomo was. There was a whispered conversation in the background, about whether the child should be given a cup of tea before she headed for a village so far away. A woman's voice hushed the whisper, discouraging them from getting involved. I heard a remark, "There will be no end to it," as I closed the door behind me. A somewhat embarrassed older man walked out with me pointing in a general direction away from the hospital and said that's where I should go. I only saw a distant mountain range where he pointed.

I started to walk away from the crowd of people and off the highway to a small, mud-caked path along rows of rice fields. I felt alone, hungry, exhausted, and very anxious. Finally, I said to myself "I can't go on anymore." I decided to sit on a cool patch of clover and wild grasses for a rest. The soy beans were too tough for my still aching teeth, but they were the only food I had. I kept them in my mouth until they were softened by my saliva and swallowed them slowly. When my hand was emptied, I was still hungry.

I put my fingers in the grass, combing through the cool, thin blades as I looked up to the sky. It was a beautiful blue, against which thick and thin white cotton clouds were moving gently across the sky, like any other summer day before. They were a familiar sight, associated with happy times, outings, running and laughing with friends and family.

Out of nowhere, something inside of me started to say, "You are on your own now. Get up Hideko, only you can make it happen." I couldn't give up. I was going to find Tomo Village no matter what it took, and I was going to be reunited with my mother there. I was certain. She would be so proud when she found out about the long journey I made all by myself. I rose on my sore feet and began walking with strength I didn't think I ever had.

After about a mile, I came upon a small stone bridge at a fork in the road. A man with a tweed beret was walking towards me from the opposite direction, pushing a bicycle. I hesitated, but was in desperate need of some direction. I mustered enough courage to ask him which road I should be taking to get to Tomo.

He was startled at being approached at first, but listened with a concerned expression to my question. He thought to himself, and then said that he could show me the long road ahead, but doubted that a child could get there before sundown. He asked, "But why do you have to go there?" I told him that I thought my house had been directly hit by the bomb, and though I didn't know what was happening all over town, there were people hurt badly, burned and bleeding, and Tomo was where my mother said our block was assigned to go.

He was shocked. He said he had heard about something happening in Hiroshima, but didn't know that it was so bad. I told him about the continuous explosions going on, and that I was terribly worried about my family. He looked at me thoughtfully, and suggested my coming with him and staying with his family for now. He was a stranger out of nowhere, but I thought that perhaps Mama would understand if I started for Tomo early tomorrow. I decided to trust my instinct that this was a genuinely kind person, willing to rescue me from the ordeal of endless walking at night.

We walked another mile. I followed the gentleman, limping and hobbling from time to time. He stopped outside a large, white wall with a temple-style gate, surrounding a handsomely built farmhouse with a beautiful dark tile roof. Pointing to it with a smile, he invited me inside. His sister-in-law, and the mistress of the house, greeted us as we entered the gate. She had a kind and round smiling face, with small eyes. He spoke in a small voice, putting his head close to her ears, explaining the situation. Nodding her head, she took me in immediately.

The mistress of the house listened closely to my story, commenting on how difficult and scary all of this must have been for a mere child, and said that she had two young daughters, one assigned to military headquarters near Hiroshima Castle in the city, and the other, a student, working in a factory just outside the city. She hoped they'd be home soon themselves. Her worried face corresponded with my anguish for my mother and the rest of my family.

I joined the family table for a hot meal of white rice with soup and vegetables, a meal I had not expected at the end of this day. After a nice hot bath, the mistress helped to clean my cuts, and provided me with a fresh bandage. A soft cushy futon was laid out for me to sleep on, with a mosquito net for nightfall.

The first daughter to return safely was the student factory worker. She was exhausted, but without injury, much to her mother's delight. Her observations and reports picked up along the way dampened her mother's hope for the other daughter's safety. The mistress was tearfully repeating to herself that she would wait up for her.

Late into the night, there was a stirring at the entrance, and the sound of excitement followed. The daughter from the military command post near Hiroshima Castle finally reached home. Badly bruised and swollen across her forehead, she had walked all the way in her torn clothing to the outskirts of the city and hitched a ride as I had.

She lost consciousness when she was in the underground command post of the Hiroshima Division of the Imperial Army, and the horrendous explosion knocked out the thick sealing door to the bunker. She did not know how long she had been unconscious, but when she regained consciousness, she staggered out with a head injury. She saw the supreme commander of the group on the floor, pale and lifeless, although not clearly injured. She talked about the soldiers and civilians being burned, their agony, and their melting, singed flesh. She was certain that she would not have come home alive if she had worked above the ground. Hobbling through the fires and dying people, she finally made it home.

The mother was ecstatic to see her last missing daughter. As the girl pointed in the direction from which she had come and the horrible sights and sounds all three of us left behind, everyone stood outside, solemnly facing the city.

The sky over Hiroshima was burning in bright orange and yellow against the dark night. How could anyone's parents or children have survived such a fire? My heart was racing and sinking deeper at the same time, despite my bliss over being rescued by this kind family.

The next morning, the farmer who brought me to his house offered to bicycle into Hiroshima to find my parents, and he urged me to hold off my trek to Tomo Village. I described in detail where our house stood. He said he was familiar with it and that he thought he could find it. He wore a glove on one hand that never came off. I guessed that under the glove was a prosthesis. I wondered if that was why he was not on the war front and, if so, I was most grateful for it. He took off early on his bike. When he returned at the day's end, he came with news of finding my father on the site of my home, but also said that my mother had not come home.

Papa had made it back just as the last section of the house was coming down in flames. He had walked for hours pushing his bike, and sometimes carrying it on his shoulders. When he finally reached our home, he saw a sign listing three missing persons, Kimiko, Hideko, and young Hideyuki. He feared both his wife and his only child had perished, his having witnessed the condition of the people who were in the city that day.

The farmer bringing the news of my being alive reached him just then. He was most grateful. I was grateful to know my father was safe and sound, but the uncertain fate of my mother left me feeling very heavy. I wondered if Mama had made it to Tomo ahead of me, and if I shouldn't try to get there myself. I would have done so, had it not been for my father's message that I was to join the rest of my relatives now taking temporary refuge on a mountain top in Kabe, some fifty miles away.

I learned that my uncle, aunts, grandmother, and baby Kumiko, miraculously escaped in time and found a place to stay, with the help of Hisao's former employee. They thought I had wandered off by mistake and was left behind. They were relieved to see me alive. When I joined the family, the number grew to six people, packed in a small guest room of a wealthy farmer, on a slope of the Uebara district in Kabe township.

Suddenly, in a matter of seconds, our home life became confined to a tiny room with a charcoal burner outside. No more long corridors lined with spacious rooms, and views of vast tranquil gardens. No more domestic help and grand catered parties. There was not even the luxury of running water which we had always had. Now, our water was borrowed from a well in the farm house, and our washing was done at a spring down the mountain path.

Uncle Hisao was bandaged up and resting. He had been able to survive only because he had run into a surgeon friend, Dr. Ikeda, who patched him up and tried to take out more glass pieces from his body. There were still a few more shards of glass left under his skin that Dr. Ikeda could not remove. Grandma Tamano and Aunt Kiyoko bore bruise marks over their faces and limbs, but were recovering as well. Because they were all inside at the time of the explosion, none of them suffered severe burns.

The very next day, Uncle Hisao, Aunt Fumiko, with Cousin Kumiko strapped on Aunt Fumiko's back, and I began trekking after the missing family members, my mother and young Hideyuki, Uncle Hisao's only son.

The stories from others who went to look for their relatives were most disturbing. We had heard that the dead and the dying were left on the ground where they fell. Rotting corpses were said to be everywhere. Those who had severe burns on their faces were hard to identify, even when they somehow survived long enough to reach a rescue station. The so-called "rescue" stations were filled to their capacities with injured but lacked medicine or aid.

Since the injured people had fled in all directions, and the city no longer existed, there were no clues even as to where to start. The newspaper informed us that the horrific destruction was accomplished by a single bomb. It said that this bomb was so lethal that Hiroshima would not be fit for habitation for the next seventy-five years.

The news did not stop anyone from going back into Hiroshima, however. People looked for their family, children, mothers, fathers, aunts and uncles, and brothers and sisters. No one could stay away, knowing that their child or mother may be dying without their comfort or help. The few lucky people who did find their relatives grieved even more deeply, since they were unable to save or relieve the suffering of the dying family members.

We began our search for my mother and Hideyuki by checking

out the local rescue stations where the injured had been carried, the schools, police yards, and temples. On our first trip to the police yard, my eyes caught a naked young woman scantily covered by a thin blue cloth, lying on the ground. "How embarrassing it must be for this girl," I thought.

Her petite body was curled up, and she was breathing with great difficulty while trying to say something. As my eyes traveled down, I saw a tag pinned to the blue cloth identifying the girl's name. She was a kindergarten teacher from our neighborhood. I tried to say something like, "Are you all right?" Breathing with a great effort, she whispered in a barely audible moan, "It's so hard, . . . it's so hard." Her body began to shake and convulsed. Then, it stopped. She died before my eyes. There were no marks on her body, no cuts or blood or burns. It was terrifying. I never saw anyone die in front of me like that in my life before, and I didn't know what killed the young teacher, either.

The next temple housed sixty or more people inside the large chapel, which resembled the temporary living quarters we had had in Kimita Village. The singed and blackened bodies were lying on the floor unattended. Those who had someone looking after them seemed just as helpless. The stench of rotting flesh filled the air. Soft moans and blinking eyes were signs of life in the dark and desolate temple hall. Shutters had been removed, and there were no windows or screens, but the sunlight did not come inside. I heard from other adults that the maggots were moving in on the dead flesh of the burn victims while they were still alive, adding to their excruciating pain.

I called out Mama's name, "Is Mrs. Kimiko Tamura here? Please answer me, please." It was very difficult to think of Mama lying there, one of these disfigured, helpless people. The only thought that pushed me on was that I could not leave her dying alone anywhere without me.

The sound of someone coming by stirred people to ask for help, and water, "Please give me water." But I had no water to give. I wanted to, and I would have if only I could. I was sorry that I couldn't give even just water. It was not much to ask for, but I was also truly afraid to be near them. A person had just died in front of me, and I was very shaken. It was horrifying to walk in and out of such painful places drenched in the smell of rotting flesh and death.

I could not bear the thought of not being able to do anything for Mama or even get to her at all. All I could do was to keep on walking to the next station. I decided to sing Mama's favorite lullabies and melodies that we used to sing together. It was as if Mama could hear me before I could find her, to be with and comfort her. I prayed, "Please God, let the wind carry the tunes to my Mama, if she is anywhere suffering, please give her comfort. Please don't let her die alone suffering." As I let the wind carry the melody of my soft humming, tears began to roll down my cheeks. I wept as quietly as possible so the wind would not carry the sound of my sobbing as I walked on to the next yard.

Uncle Hisao and Aunt Fumiko had no luck finding their son Hideyuki, either. Kiyotsune, a second cousin and classmate of Hideyuki, was found on the front yard of the Red Cross Hospital by his parents. He died a few days after his parents found him. There was nothing anyone could do for him. Kiyotsune's mother confided to Fumiko, "You may be lucky, you didn't have to watch your son's end, . . . and you won't keep on seeing how he had to die." Tomoko, another of my second cousins and a playmate, was a chubby, good-hearted girl of the clan. Tomoko never came home. She was never found. Her mother never came out of mourning and went into seclusion for the rest of her life.

Most of Hideyuki's friends from the Hiroshima First Middle School were either dead or missing, and no one had any information about their fate. Many were crushed under the collapsed classrooms, while others were scorched in the melting heat of the radiation.

One day, the lament of Kiyotsune's mother became a reality for Uncle Hisao and Aunt Fumiko, when one of their son's classmates, Hara, told Aunt Fumiko he had seen Hideyuki within hours after the bomb explosion.

Hara had managed to crawl out from under the collapsed school building because his seat was by the window, and it was easier for him to get outside than for others. He looked around for others, but there were only a few who managed to come out. Hara fled the fires by following a crowd of people moving toward Mt. Hijiyama, when he thought he recognized a back view of Hideyuki's head, but the rest of the boy's body including his face was burned beyond recognition. Hara called out to his friend, "Aren't you Tamura?" The boy was walking awkwardly in a ghost-like posture, with his hands raised before him. He responded that he was Tamura.

His burnt body was naked down to his calf girdle and army boots which he had worn with pride. Just then, they heard people hollering "The planes are coming back," so they had to run. Hideyuki told Hara that he couldn't make it anymore and to please go ahead without him. Hara saw Hideyuki collapse to the ground. Hara had to keep running, leaving his friend lying on the ground.

Hara was beginning to lose his eyesight by then, but he was able to take Hisao and Fumiko to the very spot where their only son fell to the ground. The bodies had been cleared and no trace of him remained there. They asked around if anyone might have noticed a body lying there, but no one knew about that specific one. People said there were too many bodies and the soldiers had hauled them away. No one knew where the bodies were cremated. It could have been anywhere.

This was an unbearable, yet common story for parents and children alike, except that this thirteen-year-old boy was the only son and heir, the pride and joy of Uncle Hisao and Aunt Fumiko. He was my cousin who grew up with me like a brother. He was a friend and teacher who loved sports and loved watching airplanes, Japanese and American planes alike. His being burned alive, and suffering without his family's help was so difficult to accept that no one talked about it even after we found out what had happened. I knew, however, that my aunt suffered every day of her life after learning about her only son's end. Tens of thousands of people mourned in a similar way for very similar reasons.

Another revelation came to us one day about Mama. A neighbor was found in early September who was with Mama at the moment the bomb exploded. Mama and this woman were inside a concrete building where the others had left their lunch boxes. This location was near the center of the city.

Mama had suffered a miscarriage in July, and her neighbor had two small children with her, so the two were excused from outside work. They were chatting inside at an entrance way when the bomb exploded. The woman told us that Mama pulled her straw hat down over her ears, and ran inside screaming, as the concrete building came crashing down on her. The neighbor woman stayed by the door, hovering over her two children. She lost consciousness for a short time but came to when she heard voices shouting for anyone alive. She called out in response and was dug out with her children. She called out for my mother several times before they had to leave because a fire was closing in. The woman thought there were others in the building as well, but she and her children were the only ones rescued.

Though ailing and frail herself by this time, the neighbor took Papa to the site of the building. The burned down ruin was untouched. There were several remains, so he could not tell which one may have been his wife. Then he stumbled on an army canteen he recognized as his. He had loaned it to Mama. Next to it were half-burnt and partially weathered remains. He felt Mama was calling him to notice her.

He brought home Mama's ashes in his army handkerchief. He also brought a little of others' ashes, for their families had not known to come for them, and he wished them to rest in peace as well. I begged Papa to take me back to the very place where the bones were found and collected. Despite my pleas, my wish was not granted, not until long after the building debris and the remains had been cleared. He said it was not a sight for me to remember. I failed to accept the fact that I should not see my mother in any form, but then, perhaps he was right.

I kept asking myself, "Was she crushed instantly? Did she suffer in the melting heat?"

I thought time and again, "Mama, if I only knew where you were, I would have gone through hell to get to you, and would die with you if I couldn't get you out." But I didn't. I couldn't. I was powerless. I could not accept the verdict. The most horrible indictment behind all my grief was the fact that I had insisted on coming back to Hiroshima, in spite of my mother's wish to stay one more day in Kimita Village so they could rest up. I could not face this awful thought or tell anyone that my childish desire brought her to her death. I waited for her to come home, for days, months, and years. I wonder if I ever stopped waiting.

In the city of Hiroshima and in the surrounding small towns, stacks of smoke waved in the wind from the banks of the Ota and her sister rivers for weeks on end. The pyre of the deceased was ascending to the sky leaving behind those still dying, both physically and mentally because of what they saw and breathed.

On the afternoon of August 15, the people of Uebara and the refugees from Hiroshima listened to the static-ridden, recorded radio announcement from the Emperor. Their heads were bowed to the *tatami* mats for the sound of his "holy" voice. I could not make out the words or understand them. The adults who did understand, told me that the war had ended. We had all been told to endure and keep our heads up, for the suffering would end upon the news of victory. The new suffering, however, had only just begun.

7

Lost in the Country

On the way down to the stream for daily wash-ups, I usually passed a shack about the size of a chicken coop. I seldom noticed anything different about it, but on this day, there was quite a bit of commotion and I heard loud voices shouting and wailing. The spoken words did not quite register any meaning, and I realized it was another language. Mr. Hashimoto, our landlord, explained that his Korean tenant had had a death in his family.

The tenant's brother had survived the bomb explosion earlier. He was badly injured, and just didn't make it. The family's reaction to his death was very striking. In contrast to conduct customary to usual funerals, in which mourners grieved privately, the members of this family and their friends were very open about their grieving. Their wailing, *"Aigo, aigo,"* could be heard on the mountain top long into the night. It made sense to me that one should cry out when circumstances were horribly sad.

People were beginning to hear similar stories nearly every day about someone they knew who was dying. The oddest accounts were those of people with very minor injuries, who suddenly began to vomit and bleed from their gums and other orifices until they died. This manner of suffering was like no other illness known before. The afflicted lost their strength very rapidly and died in extreme agony. To watch the process was incredibly terrifying to the family. They spoke of red spots that appeared on the body, marking the beginning of this mysterious cycle. People began checking their bodies for conspicuous marks every day, even a bad mosquito bite evoked fear.

In mid-August, I was sent down to Dr. Ikeda because I was covered with a skin infection. The cramped quarters at the top of a small mountain felt very far from the bottom when walking back up again. My legs looked like those of reptiles in our lost garden. I started to count the lesions on my legs, but lost count at seventy-five. As soon as my boils turned to dry scabs, by the end of August, chronic malaise and fevers set in.

Climbing back the uphill path with a fever was exhausting. Finally, I couldn't even walk downhill. The fever kept rising until I became delirious, oblivious to my surroundings. I felt very hot all over, as if my skull were engulfed in a shiny white light. I lay on my futon feeling very ill, but not really caring if I lived or died. I had not cried after my mother's death, discovering for the first time, that the most grievous tears were very dry, as if there were no place for them to flow. Deep within my heart was a gnawing feeling that I not only had left my mother and other injured persons behind, but was also responsible for her death. It was as though my existence lost its value entirely because of wrongdoings for which there was no expiation. I felt so profoundly shaken by the thought, that I could hardly speak of it with anyone as I lay in fever.

Sometime at the height of this calamity, I heard the whispering voices of my family in the background. Papa had been called back to my bedside. He had been detained in the army to dismantle the military and clear the corpses and debris from the city. The extensive responsibilities kept him away for months before he could come home to his child. But now, the family told him I was gravely ill. He took a temporary leave to be with me, hoping to help turn my illness around.

His youngest sister, Yoshiko, had just arrived from Kotohira on the Island of Shikoku. She brought with her a special cure: a live snapping turtle. Papa was to sever its head, while Aunt Yoshiko was to hold a cup underneath to catch the fresh blood as it dripped. I heard a commotion, apparently caused by the turtle not so willing to part with its head. Shortly after, however, a decanter full of red liquid was forced into my mouth. I was held up at a slanted angle, and Papa's firm instruction that I must drink it to live, kept me from spitting out the vile tasting liquid. Aunt Yoshiko urged a second cup, but I shook my head knowing I couldn't keep another sip down.

The next morning found the fever going down and I even had an appetite for the first time. A bowl of sweet wheat paste, *mugikogashi*, went down easier than the turtle blood. I began to eat some more and my father returned to the army the following day more confident of my recovery. There were several servings of turtle soup afterwards, made with the poor creature from Kotohira.

A few weeks later, I was up and about again. The recovery seemed slow and temporary. I did not feel like my old self. Apparently many people who survived the explosion felt the same way. I heard them complain about feeling sluggish and tired all the time.

A few months later, I became sick again to no one's surprise. This time I was jaundiced, turning yellow in the whites of my eyes. Chronic fatigue and fever persisted, so that walking up and down the mountain path to attend classes, and keeping up with studies, was no longer possible. About all I could manage was to take a few steps outside sometimes to sit on a grass patch where Mr. Hashimoto's cow was tied to a post. There was no one else to talk with and tell how lonely and weak I felt. I tried to whisper songs of my childhood, just to reach out, maybe even to spirits in the air. From time to time, a sudden and loud moo broke the monotony. Slowly, I became a silent child asking for nothing and expecting very little.

The mood of the people in general was very subdued as we continued to exchange the news of others who did not survive. The common exchange was often like, "Oh, did you know (he/she) didn't make it? Good people seem to go." Grandma Tamano, who had been known to speak her mind, was heard one day saying, "They make it sound like we who survived are bad people." We laughed and agreed with Grandma that perhaps she had a point.

It was not until the fall of that year that Papa was able to finish all his duties. After the Occupational Army had landed in Atsugi Air Base, and its contingencies had advanced to their area, Papa was made responsible for turning over to the Occupational authority all of the hidden ammunition from secret caves along the Inland. The demise of his superiors in the bomb explosion left him with tasks beyond his ordinary duties as a captain.

By this time, people were beginning to feel more relaxed about the Occupational Army. Before their arrival in Atsugi, Uncle Hisao had gathered all the women of the household, assuring us that if the soldiers came to touch any of us, he would take charge of helping us to die by our own hands first. We were prepared to commit suicide before he would let any of the soldiers touch us.

The dreadful plan proved quite unnecessary, as I came to know first-hand on my way home from school one day. I was making a usual turn into a hillside, when my heart almost stopped as I spotted a very strange person, in a khaki uniform, approaching my direction. There was no time for me to hide or run, so I just froze. The young blue-eyed soldier smiled and waved at me and went away, whistling a tune. My first encounter with a live former enemy was promptly shared with everyone back at the house.

Not all of our encounters ended as happily. Grandma Tamano's widowed daughter, Aunt Tokuko, from Grandmother's first marriage had three children, including a young son in his early twenties. He was a sweet and gentle young man, with an almost effeminate quality about him. They lived in the town of Kure, where a Navy contingent was stationed. He was delighted to find a job at the base to help support his mother and sister. Jobs were hard to come by, then, and people were going hungry every day. He used to bring Grandma Tamano and his relatives rare treats, such as chocolates, and cigarettes for his uncles. They especially loved the canned army rations.

One day Grandmother was shocked with news that her grandson

had taken his own life in the middle of the night. Aunt Tokuko had noticed that her son had come home very troubled that night. Not his usual open self, he had difficulty talking about what had happened. He simply said something awful had happened at work, and that he could do nothing to prevent it from happening again. She concluded that something had been done to her son by his foreign superiors that he was powerless to protest. She said he was frightened and apologetic about his predicament, as he knew his mother depended on his income. He did not awake from his sleep the next morning.

Aunt Tokuko wept as she told the story. She did not think that she ever wanted to see or touch any more goods from the base. Grandma's heart must have ached in sadness as she spoke and remembered my young step cousin, who had a deep love for his family, and was so terrorized that he could not face himself again. We never spoke of the newcomers at the Kure base after this incident.

There were, however, benefits that came from the Occupational Army via occasional food and health aids. We received a small amount of refined wheat flour from time to time, which we used to make dumpling soup. Another bucketful of powder, called "DDT," was for our bodies we were told. Almost all who became refugees had limited washing and laundry facilities and our clothes began to be infested with lice. The DDT was to be generously poured on our clothes and even on our bodies nightly. No one suspected, then, that what could kill an insect might also be harmful to humans.

Papa, in the meantime, was fearful of being sought out as a war criminal because of his position coordinating military supplies through the Inland Sea port. He told the family that he might have to go into hiding, for he would not allow himself to be taken prisoner.

Pointing to a shiny handgun, he indicated his resolve in the event of capture. To me, the chilling thought of being left alone with an extended family whose ways were so different from my parents was unthinkable. I thanked God the summons never came.

Before he was officially discharged from his military duties, Papa had the help of his crew to bring back a large supply of food: white rice, miso paste, shoyu, sugar, and salt, items that every household sought. The family in Uebara had been feeding on rationed food, resembling caked vomit from cows. We usually looked at each other waiting for someone to taste it first to see if it was safe to put in our mouths. Aunt Kiyoko took the first bite as we watched her swallow the brownish green stuff. She remarked that the taste was not as foul as it appeared. The rest of us followed her sampling, drinking a lot of hot tea to wash it down with. After Papa's return, we feasted on normal meals for a long while.

The daily life was hard, but newspapers came out everyday by then, bringing auspicious reports of the many changes under General MacArthur. Grandmother called him, "Matsukasa-san," pronouncing his name like her favorite kind of mushroom. For this family, the general had no impact, including on the second son, Jiro, who would have stood to gain his share of his late father's massive fortune under the new constitution. But the new order came too late. His elder brother inherited all before the war ended. No one criticized MacArthur or his staff. It was just as in the former days of the military leadership, only in a different uniform. People were accustomed to authority.

As soon as Papa came home for good, Uncle Hisao persuaded him to commute back to Hiroshima by bicycle some thirty or more miles daily, to reconstruct the family business. They left before sunrise and returned to the country late after dark.

Knowing how eagerly I waited for his return, Papa whistled a tune to me as he came around just below the farm house, signaling that he was home. I usually ran out to greet him, like a faithful canine, and was just as happy. Papa tried to take care of me whenever he could. I remember that he treated my hair when lice were discovered. He used to even cook gourmet dishes that Aunt Kiyoko or Grandma did not know how to prepare. He said that he had learned it in Tokyo, and in the army when he was stationed in China. I felt very safe whenever he was with me.

Traveling many miles daily, without adequate rest, took its toll on Papa in different ways. Late one night we were awakened by cries of intense pain. My Papa, a grown man, was curled up and shouting in agony. His elder sister, Kiyoko, was sure it was caused by the half spoiled sake she warmed for his supper earlier. His pain seemed so extraordinary that Aunt Kiyoko believed he was dying. She clasped her hands together begging for his forgiveness and hollering her apologies to him.

A doctor was sent for from the town of Kabe, at the foot of the Uebara Mountains. It took an interminably long while for help to arrive because of the distance from downtown Kabe to the desolate mountain top. After a long wait a doctor arrived. A shot of morphine did its work immediately. His spells returned time and again, but they were less frightening, knowing he was not convulsing to death. The doctor thought it might be my father's gallstones. He said there was not much that could be done about it, but that they might go away in time. After several years, the spells went away.

Another scary time for us came when I was called away from school, told that Papa had an accident and was unconscious. In the spring, a flood had washed out a bridge, forcing Uncle Hisao and Papa, who was riding ahead, to take a detour. Uncle Hisao was distracted momentarily and the front wheel of his bicycle caught Papa's back wheel pushing Papa's bicycle off the make-shift bridge, plunging him and the bicycle into a bed of hard rocks below. I knew everyone was human and made mistakes, but I loathed this one. Papa gained consciousness but suffered from nausea and a headache. However, he did not rest for long before he returned to the factory site in Hiroshima. They were reconstructing the plant, and his elder brother needed him to be there.

The news that my widowed maternal grandmother, Tome, in Kurashiki, had contracted cancer of the stomach reached us also, in the fall. Young Uncle I-chan and Aunt Kozu-chan were barely keeping up with looking after themselves. Papa was deeply concerned, so he took me to see Grandma Tome a couple of times. I sang songs about mothers, and how precious they are, like the sun, the moon, and our very lives. Grandma Tome was very quiet in her bed, but I saw her crying, without a sound.

She was thinned to the bones the first time, and later, when we returned, she was swollen as the cancer spread. It must have been very difficult for my aunts and uncle to watch their only parent wither away, as life was so stressful for them already.

Back in Uebara, my aging Grandma Tamano and Aunt Kiyoko, a twice-married but childless widow, were struggling, having been reduced to leading a very modest life in cramped quarters. Having lost most all of their belongings, even coiffeur accessories like wigs, Grandma and Aunt Kiyoko had suffered unspeakable humiliation. They had few changes of clothes, and had to present themselves with nearly bald heads. I had not seen them without their wigs before. They had to flee without them, and such items were not sold immediately after the war. Life was very hard for my grandma and my aunt, especially in those days.

Their authority as head women of the household was lost with the disappearance of our home in Hiroshima. There was no domestic help nor were there any daughter-in-laws to wait on them as they had been so accustomed to in the past. Aunt Fumiko was no longer a mousy servant, as she was in the old house. She was the wife of the clan heir, and its chief. Her husband's words were final, and she was now a major influence.

The life in a tiny room in Uebara for all of us came to an end before the first anniversary of the demise of Hiroshima. Our landlord's first son was getting married, so we had to vacate the guest room. Uncle Hisao and his family moved to another house further down the mountain road. The house belonged to an elderly woman, with flying white hair and a flair for pronouncing vegetables by "correct" names.

She insisted *tomato* was pronounced "toh-MAY-toh," and told everyone she had once farmed in America where she learned to speak English. She had not heard from her son since he had been sent to the Pacific front and had gone missing in action. She was waiting for her loved one's return like thousands of other families.

Aunt Fumiko was very tender towards her, and they seemed to share a very special sympathy for each other.

Grandma Tamano and Aunt Kiyoko asked Papa and me to remain with them, though I am not sure why they wanted the burden of having a teenaged granddaughter. Papa was their son and male protector, but I was much like his late wife, spirited and different from the people of their world. There was very little in common between us. It was as if we thought and spoke different languages. I was always identified with Mama's urban and Western values, at which my grandmother and my aunt were more inclined to poke fun than to take an interest. We ate together and I did my chores. Little interest was shown in my activities or school events. It was like living in isolation without visible walls or barriers.

Aunt Fumiko's place was definitely more open to talking and laughing. She had to keep up with her chores, but Aunt Fumiko always listened to me. She would remember from time to time the vows she exchanged with my mother, that if anything happened to either of them, they would take care of the other's child. On the other hand, I always sensed that there was something that kept us apart, that somehow I was a painful reminder of her young son, who was taken away from her in a very cruel way.

Even after a bout with a long illness, no one came to my graduation from the elementary school, or to the Arts Fest to see the plays I labored many hours to put together for the parents after the ceremony. Singing the words of our farewell to teachers and school mates, I remembered how my mother had wanted me to do my best and to work harder. "Mama, I finally did it," I said in vain, but it was too late for her to be able to see it happen. No one was there to congratulate the comeback efforts I had put forth to survive in my changed world. My wish for someone to be there on that day lingered, and all of my achievements thereafter never mattered nearly so much again.

In the spring, I entered the Kabe Girls' School, after passing their entrance examinations. They were easy in 1946. For example, one of the questions was, "How many flower petals are there in a cherry blossom?" This, of course, depended on the kind of cherry. The common Japanese species has five petals, but other equally beautiful kinds have more. The ambiguity begged for questions, but I chose the common answer, trying to think like others, where "common" was more acceptable than "individual" differences.

The newly revised textbooks were printed on the poorest quality paper. They were easily frazzled, and the books were stapled rather than bound. They were still a great improvement over the old textbooks that we had to paint over with black ink, leaving only a few pages which we were allowed to use. The teachers said it was by the order of General MacArthur and the Occupational Army, which disallowed most of the contents of our old textbooks. Anything that had remotely to do with patriotism or warrior's codes were not to be seen or read.

Despite the rugged exteriors, the content of the new texts were actually quite exciting. The history of Japan was being reintroduced in place of mythical creation. Papa was willing to subscribe to children's journals and books for me, just as my mother had done earlier in Hiroshima. The door to the wonders of the world was being opened again before my eyes. I was reading about the primitive Japanese inhabitants and the evolution of their culture, lethal diseases, and the new laws being written and why.

I found a small bookstore on my way to the school. There was only a space about the size of a small bathroom where the patrons could stand around browsing, but the place was a gold mine for book lovers. A large number of used books were on the shelves for rent at minimal daily charges. It was to one's advantage to read as speedily as possible, so the charges would stay minimal. The owner was a frail-looking long haired middle-aged man, who knew exactly where all of his books were in his huge collection. One day after an introduction to Shakespeare by a narration of *The Merchant of Venice* in Japanese by a well-known playwright, I stopped in the store to browse through the Shakespeare collection. The owner was very pleased with my inquiry, offering his favorite Shakespeare plays. He took it upon himself from then on to tutor me in the great books of the East and the West. I read voraciously, like drinking from an oasis after being rescued from a scorching desert, with a book in my hand everywhere I went.

I freely shared my newly acquired knowledge of literature with my classmates, who actually were more interested in the fashions of hair ribbons and gossip. Sometimes I found teachers quoting wrong information which I could not help but question. My questioning was not a gesture of ill-intention, but of a burning desire for truth and facts. I learned, however, there was limited encouragement for seeking the truth or new knowledge; rather, we were encouraged to do what we were told to do. I wondered if Mama wouldn't have stood behind intellectual accuracy in learning.

School life in the country among pubescent girls was actually more complicated than seeking truth and excelling in studies. The Seibi Academy had been demolished in the bomb destruction and was permanently closed upon the dissolution of the military establishment. The teaching and training in my new public schools were quite different. The students were also diverse in backgrounds in the public system, and it was difficult to know what was expected of me at any given time. I kept active in sports, art, classroom activities, and was often elected to be an officer in the student council.

I also found myself being accused and criticized for actions I had not taken part in. They ranged from passing notes in class that I hadn't written, to having rendezvous with young boys of whom I had no knowledge. We had been taught to guard our reputation since early on. "What would the neighbors say?" was taken far more seriously in Japan than it is in this country. People conducted business based on trust and the reputation was the single most important feature sought even by marriage go-betweens. For a young girl to be the subject of rumors as I was threatened serious future consequences even though the rumors were untrue. Interest in the opposite sex was the farthest thing from my mind, but a detailed account by a "witness" circulated, and no amount of protest could stop the generation of new sightings.

During a kimono sewing class which was usually slow and

unexciting to most of us, someone had passed a note with a drawing of a mouse. The teacher, Ms. Komatsu, discovered the note and considered the likely suspect to be a good drawer. All eyes turned in my direction and I became the recipient of her reproach.

One of the most painful and humiliating experiences for a Japanese student was to be reprimanded by her teacher who was usually given the utmost respect. The only thing worse than that was to be reprimanded by the teacher publicly in front of her classmates. I sat frozen in my seat at first. Mustering all the courage I could gather I stood up to appeal to the teacher and the class that I felt very hurt and troubled by this and other false accusations and to please put a stop to them.

The teacher, Ms. Komatsu, startled by my unrepentant response turned quite red and told us she needed to confer with the rest of the faculty about my request. Swishing her navy blue *hakama* (a skirt worn over a kimono) she walked out briskly. I thought mistakenly that the rumors would be put to rest finally. An hour or so later, she returned much calmer and composed. She informed us that the consensus of the faculty was that "where there is no fire there is no smoke," so that I was to conduct myself with greater circumspection.

The old saying erred in these instances, but I was defenseless. There was no one who would stand up on my behalf and defend my innocence, or teach me how best to discourage unwanted actions by others. Not having a mother meant I was without an advocate or a mentor. It meant giving up social protection I had not even realized that I had until I lost it. It was one more way the feeling of abandonment swept through my already shattered self, causing me to feel that there was not a person left who believed in me.

I felt like I was a lump or a mole sometimes, being wished away without being told so. Something inside me was starting to give way: I turned from a bubbly, curious, outgoing, and sturdy person into a defenseless and easily bruised victim, prone to retreat. From time to time, I still enjoyed organizing with other students for school plays I helped to produce, or gabbing with the other girls. But a sense of joy did not accompany these activities. I was good at making girls laugh. In the middle of laughing I noticed I could just as well turn it into crying and weeping, though it was always held back.

When my calligraphy and watercolors won first prize, as they did each year, and no one came to see them, I cared little if they would be terrible the next year.

My favorite activity, then, became climbing a treacherous hill with a very sharp incline, without a path. I even invited a few girls to take this task on with me. We giggled and screamed the entire time as we slid, losing our grip sometimes when footing gave way. It was a passion beyond fun loving. I wanted to keep on doing this all the time. It was one of the few times that I felt worthy as I safely made it to the top, for the danger and the challenge were both real. I easily could have slipped and met my demise.

Swimming in a rapid stream was another respite. I had no swimsuit, but used to dive and float in swiftly moving water, downstream, in my underwear. The challenge of not hitting the sharp rocks or getting sucked into the whirlpool was scary, and yet, sought passionately. The water was chilling to the bone, making my lips and finger tips shiver and shrivel in a short time. The challenge of nature was fair. The rules were laid out, and I could meet them with skill, courage, or daring.

In comparison, the challenges of life's events and people were far more unpredictable and life threatening. The coping skills of a girl without her mother's support and guidance were hardly equal to the task required. How was I to know that my entire universe was going to collapse when it did? How was I to find joy in living when there was no encouragement for trying, or praise for a job well done? How was I to defend myself against false accusations, when no one believed in me? How was I to know that there would be a better tomorrow, when today was so utterly unbearable, without a soul who really cared? By this time, my father was so exhausted by the demands of the physical reconstruction of the business that he had nothing left for his daughter.

I missed Mama more than ever. I knew she would have stood by me no matter what had happened. She would have tried to explain all the things that I had not understood. She returned to me in my dreams, though only a few times. I remember running to her and asking her, "Mama, why haven't you come home? I've been waiting for you so long. It's been so hard, Mama!" She never explained to me why she had been away in my dreams. I saw her, calm but pensive, carrying a little bundle as if she were en route somewhere. I remember shouting in excitement that my mother was found and well, and that she was coming home. My memory has become vague about her responses. In one dream she came home with me, but when I awoke she was gone. In another dream, she could not come home with me. I do not remember why she could not return.

8

The People's Hope

The prediction that Hiroshima would be uninhabitable for the next seventy-five years was never taken seriously by anyone who lived in the city either before or after the bomb. There were even some who never left the city, because of their duty to defend it like my father did, or like a few of my relatives who with the help of their employees, successfully defended their factory and houses against the inferno. Of course, it helped that there were large vacant fields around the structures, but those men were determined to die in the fire to save the plant and the owner's house next to it.

Most of us who went back into the city, either to look for our relatives, or to return to the sites of our burnt-down houses, at least breathed plenty of the contaminated air. None of us worried about it, not that we disbelieved the lethal claim, but we simply did what we had to do.

My grandfather's estate had been built originally by the Duke Uemura, whose ancestors served the Lord Mouri, the ruling House over the middle region of Japan since the sixteenth century, before the Meiji Restoration of 1867. The elevated ground was rich in vegetation, intricately landscaped around an elegant and traditional home, and fit for the man who paid the highest taxes in the entire prefecture.

The first time we returned to the ruin of our home along with my grandmother and aunts, we were speechless. We looked for something we could possibly recognize. The huge rocks in the garden lay just the same as before. Many of the evergreen trees remained, but were disappearing fast, as returning neighbors in need of firewood helped themselves. A new, tall and straggly looking plant that we had never seen before was growing all over in our gardens and along the river bank, roadside and everywhere. It was called "railway grass" for its resilience in defying death and the contaminated soil. Some people ate the leaves for sustenance, but we never tried them. Somehow, no matter how hungry we became, we did not feel up to eating plants that grew out of the bombed soil.

The place where our house had once stood was covered mostly by thick layers of broken clay roof tiles. What were once beautiful, dark gray tiles had turned into baked reddish brown pieces. Bending down and kneeling, we began to dig, looking for something that might still be saved. We kept removing one tile after another, only to see more tiles. Grandma found her rice china mostly broken to pieces. She saved a few tiny cups with cracks and brown marks. The only thing I found in the remains of my family's room was a melted sake bottle that Mama had used to refine brown rice in by pushing a wooden stick in the bottle up and down. For a few seconds I met with an image of Mama chatting with me while her hands were busy with the up and down motion, holding the bottle filled with brown rice. The house and garden that held memories of all our lives for so long were gone forever. We came back several times, but after a while, we realized that the shattered site made us long for what could never be restored to us. We stopped returning. We never again saw the beautiful insects and creeping creatures that used to roam in the gardens during the life of our old estate, after the fire.

Early in the spring of 1948, three years after our house and factory were leveled to the ground, Papa designed and built modest, small houses on the bank of the Ota River and on the original estate. By then, the plant was also rebuilt, smaller, but fully operational for manufacturing sewing needles. The rubber industry had been given to the late founder's brother-in-law, Bunji Nishikawa, whose house and factory miraculously survived the fire. The Nishikawa family continued to prosper. Papa, Uncle Hisao, and their families finally came together to live. I hoped it would work out better than living with Grandmother and Aunt Kiyoko, who had been so unhappy themselves.

There were others who had also returned to their home sites. Some of the shelters resembled piles of sheet metal put together instead of regular homes. People were short of materials for building shelters. We owned very few changes of clothing; we washed even sweaters every few days if they were light colored. All the fuzz had come off by then, but we tried to keep ourselves clean.

The scarcity of daily supplies of food and clothes was so common to everyone that we paid less attention to proper attire than would have been thinkable before the war. When the signing of the Japanese surrender on the battleship *Missouri* was first shown on film, I was awed by the pictorial reporting. I also remember wondering about how the Honorable Mr. Shigemitsu, the Japanese ambassador who signed the surrender, might have managed to locate the proper attire complete with a top hat for the occasion.

Slowly, however, one could almost feel that the people and the city were beginning to feel alive again despite the material hardships and the *bura-bura* illness, the fatigue syndrome from which the survivors often suffered.

One place that brought this feeling of returning normalcy was a cafe called *Shubo,* meaning "The People's Hope." It was run by my art teacher, Mr. Yamasaki, from my Kabe Girl's School, and his wife. He had studied painting in Paris before the war. Mr. Yamasaki used to tell me I could become an artist in the period when I was most discouraged and without hope. He liked my sketches and watercolors. I told him I would rather be a writer. He used to say that it was possible for even a woman to become both an artist and writer. I was utterly amazed how anyone could have said anything so bold and wonderful at a time when everyone was pessimistic about the future.

Papa discovered the cafe near the Yokogawa station, which was a secondary and smaller railway station for Hiroshima. The mere presence of European coffee and tea, combined with fresh baked pastries, was like being brought back to our happiest pre-war days. We listened to the music of Beethoven and Mozart while enjoying the taste of fruit pie with a fine layered crust which melted in our mouths. The cafe called "The People's Hope" was a place where we could dream again before we stepped out onto the burned and vacant soil of our hometown.

Sometime in this period or maybe it was even earlier, our "living God" the Emperor came to our desolate town. Before the reign of MacArthur, we had been prohibited from making any direct eye contact with His Holiness or the Empress. Near the Gokoku Shrine in the center of the leveled city the human Emperor climbed a few steps to a hastily constructed small wooden platform. After all the years we were taught to live and die in his name until the worst of its consequences was brought down on all of us, I had to see him. So did thousands of others who came. The former living God wore a tired, worn woolen coat and a suit, a crushed hat in his waving right hand, and was surrounded by a sea of people. I don't remember what he said or if there were words of consolation but none was necessary. We understood that his very presence was his sincere expression of regret for our plight and the plight of the country. The ground swell of *"Banzai"* was repeated spontaneously, by young and old who never expected to encounter the former God in their lifetime.

An unexpected gift in returning to Hiroshima was being close to the river. Our plant and the house were rebuilt along the Ota River, and my favorite activity became walking along the river bank, and watching the sunset. I would sit on the grass full of clover leaves and wait for the dusk to set. One day, I noticed a four-leaf clover under my finger tip. I had had no such luck before and wondered if there might possibly be another one. There was, in fact, there were tens and hundreds of other ones. The river bank, which had been trodden on by the injured and the dying not so long ago, was filled with four-leaf clovers. I was ecstatic, and collected them all evening long. The thought of mutation caused by radiation never occured to me at the time. I was searching for and found the symbol of happiness on the river bank.

In the meantime, the people of Hiroshima were being visited by a new kind of worry: a summons from the Atomic Bomb Casualty Commission, or ABCC for short. The word from a few who had been called was that the Commission was interested in observing and checking out the survivors, but was unwilling to dispense any medication. This gave rise to the perception that individuals were being used in medical research for the former enemy, but with no tangible benefit to the survivors themselves. The complaints were shared with some trepidation, since no one wished to defy orders from the Occupational Army or anything remotely connected with it.

The doctors from the ABCC, we were told, examined the patients in a drastically different manner than that followed by Japanese physicians. The female survivors were horrified when they were asked to disrobe entirely and to put on a gown. Fortunately, none of us in the family received a summons.

At home Papa tried to teach me about the peaceful use of nuclear power. I often heard him thinking out loud about the possibility of turning nuclear energy into a power source, and thereby producing electricity or anything people desired. It would still take some time, he thought, but he believed it was the right way to use atomic power. He wanted me to separate my fear of the nuclear bomb that killed my mother from the wisdom of using the same source for the betterment of humanity. He believed that it was a marvelous discovery that needed to be harnessed. I never once heard him blame the radiation for the death of his wife or the destruction of his homeland.

I could not fully understand this view. The other family members were even less enthusiastic about his ideas, treating them as another one of his complicated notions. If they never again heard of radiation or atomic power, it would have been soon enough as far as they were concerned. The *pika-don*, as Grandma Tamano referred to the bomb, was never exonerated by them.

Papa was in favor of tearing down the remains of the dome that still stood at the center of Hiroshima. I was dismayed. It was a memorial to the dead and a reminder against a future holocaust. He was adamant about the need for people's energy to be directed to the needs of today. Everyone must keep moving forward. He felt that too many people from Hiroshima were mentally trapped in death and destruction. His views felt cold and unfeeling to me, as I was not ready so soon to leave the dead behind. On this issue, we never saw eye to eye. More people were on my side.

Papa chose the Methodist mission school for my schooling in Hiroshima. It was named the Hiroshima Jogakuin, which was a consortium of junior and senior high schools and colleges. I had no special interest in education by this time. One school was as good as another. The mission school was supported by the Americans and was the first school to be rebuilt at its original site. Papa thought the new age would require an ability to speak English. He felt that a spoken language could not be mastered without exposure to native speakers. For this he felt the mission school, in which American missionaries taught, would be the best.

The first day of class in Hiroshima Jogakuin Consortium was not only awkward but confusing. Starting with the morning chapel, singing hymns, reading the bible, listening to a reflective talk, praying, and then ending with more singing and prayer, were mentally overwhelming, for there were no experiences corresponding to these practices from my past. At the close of the day, a student led a mini-service by choosing a hymn and giving a prayer.

I had no idea that all of these strange activities awaited the transferees. The exposure to the native speakers was just as intimidating. It started with a demanding, stern American missionary, whose native speech was too fast for me to understand. The exposure was a nightmare. I prayed a lot not to be called on by the missionary in my English classes, or to have to lead the closing prayer at the end of the day. I had never felt so incompetent.

Bible study was taught each week by a young minister who was quite a deep thinker and enjoyed questions. His style of teaching was stimulating to the mind. The Bible, however, kept me busy keeping track of so many foreign names, from one clan to another. There were even more names for the disciples of the Son of God. The hymns, on the other hand, were easier to become familiar with for a start, since I always liked singing.

In the meantime, wearing the uniform of a navy jumper over a white blouse, and a small pin in the shape of a shield bearing the words, "Cum Deo Laboramus," which translated as "working with God," I looked in every way like a Jogakuin girl. I was elected class leader a month after the transfer, without knowing much about anything of Jogakuin.

Moving in with Aunt Fumiko, a warm, sympathetic woman devoted to her family, was a welcomed change. She was willing to share what was left of herself with Father and me. We were grateful for her help. I did the wrong thing one day. I sketched Aunt Fumiko's profile. Aunt Fumiko hated her uneven teeth. She was very angry and very hurt. She refused to speak to me for quite a while. I wondered how Mama might have reacted. My sense of it was that she would more than likely have smiled. I should have been more sensitive to my aunt's feelings, but perhaps I was unaware of this and was testing her limit. Well, that was the limit. I found out.

Reaching physical maturity, in the summer before my first year of high school, came as a total surprise to me. Uncle Hisao was nudging his wife during dinnertime, following a questioning look in my direction. Aunt Fumiko motioned me to leave the table with her. She took me to the bathroom with a supply of cotton. She told me that I was starting to have a monthly period like a woman. The next day a red bean and rice dinner was cooked in celebration. I was never so embarrassed about my private development in my entire life.

Following this episode, Papa began considering remarriage. He was a man who had seemed committed to staying a bachelor, and who had given no indication of any matrimonial interest. He was now looking over photographs and accepting *omiai* meetings. Soon, a widow, twelve years my senior, was chosen and the matrimonial arrangements were confirmed. We were told she was a teacher in a sewing school from one of the villages outside Hiroshima. Papa was anxious for me to meet her and for us to become acquainted. We went out once. We spoke very little to each other. The meeting was deemed successful, and the wedding date was set to be held in the grand *zashiki* room of the Nishikawas.

I watched Papa and his new bride-to-be, Tetsuko-san, being wed by an exchange of wine with the blessings of the relatives. They took off on a honeymoon boat, sailing on the Inland Sea. I had very little part in these events, except to try to be fair and pleasing. I made my best effort to endear myself to my young stepmother by promising her that she might wear some of Mama's kimonos that were saved in the country, if she would like to do so.

But in reality, relationships are not formed so simply or comfortably between two personalities such as ours, where much suffering had preceded. It was difficult for Tetsuko-san to understand a young teen without having had any children to raise, and to come into a family where intimate bonding already existed between her husband and his daughter.

It might have been that both of us were caught in an impossible situation. My very presence reminded her that she was not the first wife whom Papa had loved so deeply. For my part she was not and could not be my mother. Tension began to surface between us, and she lodged chronic complaints with Papa without my knowledge. I began to feel as I did when I stood accused earlier in the country schools, defenseless and abandoned. But to keep the peace in the family, I made no protest, shrinking each day into a carcass-like existence. I had no knowledge of how to unravel the growing complications. Aunt Fumiko preferred to stay out of it. She wanted to let the new family work out its own problems. Tetsuko-san was expecting the arrival of her new baby, while my proud father was away much of the time.

As a consequence, I felt numb, as though I were a bit of vapor, without even a physical presence beginning to emerge. By becoming invisible like the air around me, I felt as if my pain would also go away, while my family and I went on about our daily business without being able to address our growing pains in a meaningful fashion.

While our family was immersed in its difficulties, I also learned that some of my classmates were also caught in a losing battle with the stressful times and circumstances. One day, walking on a downtown street in Hiroshima, I saw a news flash posted on the corner bulletin. The name "Oki" jumped out. Oki, my classmate from the Seibi Academy, and his younger sister who had attended Hiroshima Jogakuin, were strangled to death by their own father, who had been despondent over his business failure. I could not believe my eyes. The sweet little girl who was with me in Kimita Village, and the sturdy young man who made it through the war safe and sound, were gone just as suddenly as their beautiful mother, who did not survive the war's end.

Many people walked around with keloid burns, but more people were walking around with invisible scars that were just as hurtful, if not worse. In later years, I heard stories of other classmates whom I had left behind in the country. When they returned to Hiroshima with their teachers, there were a few for whom no family members were left.

One such classmate, I learned later, who was an only son of a prominent antique dealer in Hiroshima, was met by his mother who came to take him home. Their home had been destroyed by the bomb, and his father had been killed. She brought his ashes, saying, "This is your father." She was sickly and was slowly dying. Alone without adults' help, he sought food and care for her and himself unsuccessfully. When she died, this only son of the once wealthiest family in Hiroshima, who had never lacked anything before, had to go and find a wheelbarrow to take his mother's corpse, so she could be cremated along with the others piled on the river bank. He was merely a child, a sixth grader, who was never the same after this abandonment.

9

A Rainy Day in Hiroshima

Rain, rain, rain,
Black rain
Gentle rain
Rain no more

A song was floating in my head while I was idling in my chair, looking out at the wet sky. Rain drops were bursting on the cold pavement when the bell rang. The next class was tenth grade English conversation, taught by Ms. Jones, a missionary from Odessa, New York. She was short with pretty blue eyes and her hair was usually tied up in a pony tail with a striped ribbon. I really wasn't interested in being exposed to the native speakers. Instead, I dreaded them. Sitting second from the front was no advantage in this regard.

The English literature majors, girls who kept high enough grades in most subjects, were waiting in the room. Some were from the Seibi Academy days, like Teiko, who was seated just in front of my desk, wearing a permanent eye patch. I suspected she was losing her eyesight slowly. No one spoke about it, especially Teiko herself. I remembered her happy laughter like the ringing of a bell in the old days. The sound of a flowing staccato on the playground, or in classroom, during breaks, blended with my memory of the carefree days before the forced evacuation and bombing.

Teiko was evacuated to a relative's home, when both her parents were killed by the A-bomb explosion in the city. I remembered her father as a prominent doctor who was in charge of his own hospital. Teiko used to be such a merry and playful little girl. Sometimes we even collided over whose games to play. She was not the same person anymore. I miss her laughter which sounded so much like the ringing of a bell.

Of other Seibi friends that I remembered who should have been here in class today was my best friend, Miyoshi. She didn't make it in the explosion. Our promise to get back together soon was never fulfilled, since I last saw her on the fifth of August in 1945. Another who could have been here was Nishimoto, who used to play Mozart on the piano so brilliantly that even our music teacher, as I've said, lost track of time. She and her widowed mother lived near the epicenter. They never had a chance. Crisp sounds of piano keys, especially, piano concertos by Mozart, often take me back in time to the sunny music room with a grand piano, listening to our little virtuoso.

Pushing these thoughts away on a rainy day was neither hard nor easy since the wet gray mood was an anesthetic to me. My dulled spirit was watered by rain like a flower seed in dry soil, while others saw it as a minor nuisance. My grades hadn't received much attention lately, nor did my homework. These things were the least of my concern.

The sound of the door opening and closing brought silence. The former phys ed teacher, wearing her green corduroy jacket, was ready to begin looking around the classroom. I pulled my head in like a turtle. Ms. Jones asked how the class liked the rain. Soft groans went across the room and the teacher chuckled.

"I see you don't like rain. Isn't there any one who does?" she asked. A hand went up, and the question was repeated, "Why do you like a rainy day? Tamura-san?"

The sound of my name being called startled me as I realized my hand was raised, almost unconsciously. A disastrous mistake; no matter, it was too late. I hated being put on the spot, especially in English class because it always made me feel like a fool. I couldn't make the cross-over necessary to think or speak in unfamiliar words. My mind already had to stretch to make too many adjustments to things that made little or no sense to me everyday. Were it possible, it would have suited me fine to have dug a hole and stayed there like a mole without a spring shadow.

I tried to stammer out a word or two about a rainy day, that I thought better on a rainy day, but stopped trying, as I felt foolish and awkward. I blurted out the sentence by saying I couldn't possibly tell her the reasons in English, for they were too deep and complicated. Undaunted by my reply, the teacher quickly suggested that I go ahead and respond in Japanese. The minds of two determined people were coming to a near standstill. The teacher clearly had the upper hand.

When I muttered that such an exercise would be unfair to the teacher and the rest of the class during English hour, Ms. Jones answered decisively that she would have someone translate, which would be a good practice. I made one more try at being excused by saying I still would have a problem, since my thoughts could only be best expressed in poetry. It was an invitation for Ms. Jones to ask for more. The exchange made me feel like I was disrobing in public, which was grossly embarrassing. The missionary from Odessa closed the discussion by asking me to bring a poem for her next English conversation class.

I went home that day with a burden of homework that I had no choice but to produce. I knew my teacher would ask for it from me personally. I hadn't done any homework for longer than I cared to remember. No one worried about my report card. Someone always stamped a sign of family inspection. If I passed the courses, that was all that was required of me. I'd just as soon go to a movie or stop at a noodle house and chat or laugh about nothing than do homework.

I sat at my desk in my little house, by the bank of the Ota River, looking at the rain again. Misty gray air was filling the empty space between the raindrops outside the window. A poem? No sweat. But why would anyone care what I thought about anything? I was largely uncomfortable with all the attention that was focused on my responses during the class, but now, I experienced a faint satisfaction from it. Words began to emerge, which I jotted down. They were more about my own quest than reasons why I liked the rain. I do believe I was thinking about seeking truth.

Truth

Where can the Truth be?
Could it be in my heart
So worn and dirtied
Like an old apron?
Or could it be found
In a little flower by the road
Wet and frozen from the icy rain?
Surely, Truth can be found
Everywhere and yet nowhere.

There was privacy in my room. I could sit and watch the passers-by, and take out my mother's picture. The act was forbidden since my father's new marriage. He wished that I would put reminders of my mother out of sight for my new mother's comfort, especially Mama's picture. He didn't believe in reminders. He was a kind and gentle man, but he could not possibly realize how much he truly had invaded my very special domain. I had so few precious pieces of my mother left, and he was demanding that I put even these away.

I did make a protest of a sort by sending my monthly allowance of 1000 yen to a shoeshine boy, named Santa-kun, via a local newspaper. He had been featured in the paper as a guardian of homeless orphans sleeping around Hiroshima station. The paper reported that he was trying to raise money to build housing for them. He was having a difficult time. I wrote to say that I wanted to donate the money which had been saved to purchase a locket for my mother's picture. Papa was quite displeased when an article appeared later in the paper praising my contribution. My secret rendezvous with Mama in my tiny room continued while my new family was growing.

My step-brother, Hideo, had been born a year after father's remarriage. A plump and healthy boy, Hideo was strapped on my back after school. I don't really remember this at all. My friends used to say that that was how they had to visit with me, with Hideo on my back, literally. I made a knit top for him when he was born. There were no more children after Hideo.

Much to my surprise, the poem I brought to my English class the following week sparked a lively discussion in the class, after it was translated by a Nisei student. I had forgotten that there were a minority of believers in my class, who refused to give into the presence of universal untruth as I saw it. There were at least a few who admitted that all was simply not knowable. This was not correct according to the Christian students. They "knew" where the "Truth" was. They were adamant about their knowledge of the truth and made it known. The position of those students who believed that nothing could be stated in absolute terms seemed quite reasonable to me. I had come to believe that all things were in a state of flux, as life itself seemed to be defined by change.

The different perspectives coming from Christian and Buddhist backgrounds did separate our thinking, and to a great extent, our attitudes about knowing and not knowing. The girls from traditional non-Christian homes were very comfortable with a state of fluctuation and perennial changes. The Christian students put forth their conviction more intensely, defending their God and the place of Christ. They were definitely believers, and I admired their enthusiasm even though I was offended by it at the same time.

Ms. Jones listened to the arguments with amusement, and without commenting, which was refreshing. The metaphor of the poem accomplished the teacher's purpose in the end, by creating a heated and stimulating discourse.

In the end, my respect for the teacher from Odessa rose immeasurably. I remembered another English class in which students were asked to write their autobiographies. My papers were well received until I wrote about my father getting intoxicated towards the end of the war. There were red marks all over my paper with remarks that such things about one's father should never be mentioned.

Ms. Jones, on the other hand, was different from traditional missionaries. She didn't go around pushing Bible classes. She didn't seem to be afraid to talk or share her feelings with the students on any subject, at their level. Her teaching was not found in printed words, but more in her heart. It worked. Soon the girls flocked around her and laughed with her about anything, mostly little things from their hearts.

I began to look forward to being tapped by Ms. Jones. I stood by the window in the hallway, looking outside in my usual bystander stance. Our conversations had to be limited and awkward, since I had been so averse to learning a foreign language. Slowly, there were more and more words in our exchanges, and the communication began to flow. I had forgotten how I had hated making a fool of myself. I was learning to trust someone again, without even realizing it.

I don't remember when it began exactly, but there developed a special chemistry between us, and a close bond. It could have happened possibly when I asked my teacher in one of those short chats if she had anything for an empty heart. Ms. Jones invited me to her home for a supper and often for an overnight stay. We slept in the same bed like a mother and a child in a Japanese home.

Back at home, thousands of miles away, and many years before, Ms. Jones had grown up with a mother who had been orphaned early, and was lonely at heart, but loved flowers and reciting poetry. Whatever the connection, the two of us traveled together near and far, like one soul in two bodies.

I began to write in my journal about my growing affection for my teacher, calling her "Mama." I put the journal away in my drawer. A few days later, my private entry was ridiculed by an irate stepmother who resented the remark. The humiliation of being robbed of my very private possessions, and of having my revered teacher desecrated, tore my heart to shreds.

Papa was mostly passive in these affairs between Tetsuko-san and his daughter, probably because he did not want us to appear too close after my stepmother's constant tirades about the "unhealthy bond" between himself and me. He seldom backed me any more. He held me responsible for his wife's displeasure, even in her invasion of my journal. He appeared caught in the middle, becoming an ineffective form of support for his wife as well as for me.

Just as I was beginning to feel wanted and supported by another human being, more problems were created at home. I started to think of ending it all so that everyone, including myself, would have some peace.

To exit this world by actually carrying out suicide was not a very simple task. I began to focus first on why I had to do so, as no alternative solution seemed to be available. I was simply exhausted and depressed by the demands of everyone, and I seemed unable to please anyone. Differing views of life around me were equally confusing. I was reading European existentialism and the cynical depictions of an uncertain world, in which one may be turned into a giant insect or chased and accused of wrongs never committed. Nietzsche's *Thus Spake Zarathustra*, describing the sinking descent of a young man just as he aspired to climb upward, appeared to match my sentiment exactly.

I also felt very detached from the notion that one could be saved as my Christian friends believed. I felt that Christ had nothing to do with saving me from the A-bomb, the loss of my mother, my troubled stepmother, or my painfully passive father. I felt as though it all had to be my fault. I was a person with few merits, and yet according to the Bible, I was precisely the kind of person Christ would save. It had no verity at the time. I hated the foreign name "Christ" for such a crucial figure. Why couldn't it be "Taro" or "Ichiro" or even "Hanako" which would have been more akin to my life? Loving characters from great foreign literature was not quite the same as accepting them to be one's personal God and Savior. I prayed in vain. There was no relief. I remained extremely miserable.

For several days, I thought about the quickest and the surest way to end my life. I loved the dusk, just at the time of sunset each evening, and the walks by the river bank. I chose the railway bridge two blocks away for my final demise. I timed the passing trains for a couple of nights. One night, I decided on the right time period, immediately after supper. Every one would be relaxing and no one would notice my slipping away. On the night I decided to carry it out, I burned all of my intimate letters from friends so there would not be more ridiculing of my relationships. I washed and combed my long hair, and put on a clean blue cotton blouse and a tan, A-line skirt.

My heart raced a bit as I began timing myself while I headed towards the bridge. So it will all come to an end tonight, I thought. I would have been less than honest if I said there were no regrets about my decision at that time. I was choosing to die since no other options existed in my mind on that evening.

I was almost at the crossing, by then walking very swiftly, with my face tightening and my heart rate quickening. I was starting to run, so that I wouldn't change my mind at the last minute. Then, suddenly, there was a banging jolt, and the train that was heading my way stopped. There was some shouting and stirring of people gathering around the track. I did not understand. I was about to die and was stopped after coming so close to it. There was a pair of men's *getta* sandals neatly placed by the track. I had heard whispering voices from the crowd of passers-by that an old man had jumped before the train. I walked home. I told no one about the event. I imagined that I heard that old man's voice saying, "But you are still so young."

I gave up the idea of being run over by a train once the reality of such a grisly end reached me. I thought about the method of overdosing with a stimulant called Adorumu. It was becoming popular among students for its ability to help students stay awake. It was sold over the counter. A famous writer, Osamu Dazai, used it to finish himself. I bought several packets of Adorumu and kept them in my pockets, for I knew now that I had no privacy at home.

The timing of this was altogether up to me, unlike the plan that relied on the train schedule. I spent a few days thinking about sharing my departing thoughts with a good friend, Etsuko, who sensed my sentiment. When I told her of my plan, she became quite grieved. Etsuko was one of three students whose parents were displaced business executives back from China and Manchuria, after the war. There was a special kind of sensitivity these young people felt that corresponded to something within myself. They understood about one's universe collapsing and feeling as if everything was lost.

Shortly after our discussion, a thick letter from Etsuko was hand delivered to me. In it she said that I represented a form of hope as a decisive young woman, free of spirit, clear of mind and a remarkable creature. "If you have to go, what justification do I have for remaining?" she wrote. Such were words of confidence and support for all that I had tried to be, and Etsuko was saying that she recognized that and valued me for who I was. On the grass, by the pond of the Osente garden, and in the noodle shops, we talked for hours about the despair within ourselves and in the world. We also shared one soul.

While this was going on, I was also caught off guard by Ms. Jones's discovery of my Adorumu tablets in my pocket. The teacher literally grabbed them and forced them away from me. I commented that I could procure more from where they came from. Ms. Jones became very quiet, looking at me with tears in her eyes.

I learned later that Ms. Jones spoke with Papa through a middle school teacher as an interpreter about my plight. He called me to the living room, pale and shaken. I felt defenseless. He spoke while wiping away tears with his handkerchief, saying that he tried his best to care for me. The memory of his late wife was precious to him as well. I was being very difficult, and everyone was too critical, and no bride would stay with me in the household. He said that I had to change my ways and reform.

It broke my heart to see Papa so grieved. It was all I could do to hold back my own sobbing, but I managed to I listen to him without a trace of tears. I begged for his explanation of the negatives, so I might see a way of reforming. He was very vague. He thought that I should show in more ways an attempt to be in harmony with my stepmother, whatever form that may take. I was left feeling defensive and with the renewed idea that I somehow caused everyone's unhappiness, including my own. So the no-win situation was right back at my door. My father's tears became an indictment of my unlovableness instead of sympathy for my feelings of helplessness.

When I think of that dark rainy afternoon in our living room today, I wonder why I didn't break down myself and tell him just what it felt like to be in my shoes. I know he would have understood. We would at least have been authentic in accepting the tragedy of our situation. Now he has long since passed away, and I regret that I did most of the listening without being able to share my true feelings.

It was this meeting that marked the beginning of the realization that the home I had called my own was indeed disappearing, along with the support I had relied on from my father. With no more reason for me to stay, I reasoned that contrary to the custom for Japanese females, I was going to have to rely on myself if I wished to live out my life on my own terms.

In the privacy of my room, I felt as hollow inside as ever before. Without even being conscious of it I found myself putting a razor to my fingers. I was making blood stains on my notebook. It didn't hurt, no, it didn't hurt. It was like testing to see if I had any feelings left. I showed the stains to Etsuko who looked at me without too much reaction, and said there was no point in hurting myself or bleeding just for kicks. The impulse to hurt just for kicks was washed away by my friend's calm. We continued to work together. We shared our views and supported each other's interests working together on school newspapers and joining discussion groups.

Etsuko's parents' villa on Miyajima Island was a perfect haven for the two of us. Carrying a bagful of rice, we cooked, swam, walked, and sunned by the ocean with the sound of breaking waves roaring in our ears. We talked for hours, far into the night. We searched for our true worth and identities, that were somehow lost in the changing, postwar world. We never spoke of the holocaust we had each seen and lived through. I thought that Etsuko had escaped from Manchuria when the Russians overran the territory at the close of World War II. At the time, she only spoke of clutching a baby girl cousin as she fled fires caused by air raids. Later I learned that Etsuko, her mother, and her two brothers had actually returned to Japan from Manchuria before the end of the war, only to be caught in fire bombings on Shikoku Island. She never talked of the terror of her experience. I never talked of my suffering from the explosion in Hiroshima.

My earlier interest in homeless orphans also became more serious after I abandoned the idea of terminating my short life. I felt I needed to actually become more useful in the Hiroshima orphanage, which was located behind the railway station. It was called Shudo-In, a name commonly used to refer to a monastery or a cloister. The director of the nursery was a teacher in health education at our school. She agreed to let me come and work for her. Ms. Jones had helped establish a summer internship for a few students. I was placed in the nursery where there were twenty or more infants and toddlers. My job was feeding and keeping them clean. Compared to my chubby baby stepbrother, who was growing by leaps and bounds, these were frail babies, for whom there were never enough loving arms to go around.

A few of us who worked there shared passion for extending all the love and help we could give. My supervisor never seemed to tire. She held and spoke to each baby as though she/he were her very own child. She knew their personalities and their cries. She grew furious one day when one of the junior assistants propped a milk bottle in the crib for feeding. This was to be avoided at all cost. The babies were to be held and talked to, most especially when they were being fed. She was really a superior mother.

The most unforgettable image of the orphanage that comes back to me today, however, is that of a little two-and-a-half-year-old Eurasian boy, called "Henry." His features were completely Occidental, with an angular nose, wavy blond hair and beautiful blue eyes, though his mother was Japanese. He only spoke English. I heard the long wailing sounds of a child when I arrived at work one day. I learned that his adoptive parents, who had cared for him since his birth, had to leave him behind because their government would not permit Henry to enter his adoptive parents' country.

There were stuffed animals wet from his tears and other toys that had been left with him. Coming from the Mission School, I was relied on to help speak English to Henry. He would have none of it.

He missed his family, and cried for days. I don't remember when he stopped, or if I ever saw or heard him run and laugh like other children. There were more than a few toddlers who were brought to the orphanage for the same reason. They were left behind by their American parents who could not take their adoptive children home with them.

When I was not working at the orphanage, I ventured to visit young women in the tuberculosis wing at the Hiroshima Memorial Hospital. Ms. Jones was lending her active support. I brought the patients copies of my teen magazine called *Sunflower* and whatever cakes and candies I could buy with my allowance. I was an awkward visitor. I did not know quite what I should say to comfort them. I just wanted them to know that their disease did not drive me away. I felt sad and cared about their isolation.

The young women who were isolated in this ward were actually a few years older than me and were very kind and generous in accepting my intrusion in their lives. We talked about girlish concerns, like how to give facial massages for smooth, pimple-free skin, my school experiences, and their families. Some were able to leave and go home. A few became more ill and died. In this so-called contaminated city, there was a reverence for life, even for what little was left of it in this ward.

My friend, Etsuko, and I now began discussing possible plans for our future, a future which was uncertain and vague. Etsuko's parents were facing financial difficulties, as were mine. Fortunately for Etsuko, she had kept up her studies more tenaciously than I had. She was able to win a scholarship to Doshishya University without an entrance examination. I longed to join my friend, but the door to education away from my city was closed.

Papa informed me they could not afford to send me to a college outside of Hiroshima. His expenses were mounting with a new family. Gone were the days when he used to tell me that he would send me to Keio, his alma mater. When I reminded him, he simply said that times had changed, making a slurring sound with his mouth. I noticed that he began this habit when he was under stress or was annoyed.

My adult ally, Ms. Jones, was also preparing to leave the country on a furlough. She spent less and less time with me, particularly after a new American administrator arrived. Ms. Johnson was Dr. Hirose's former English teacher, whose presence was requested by the president to lend her a hand. Ms. Johnson, who was from Macon, Georgia, stayed with Ms. Jones, and they were close friends.

I understood that this was how Ms. Jones wanted it, though my understanding did not take away my feeling of loss, even before my teacher left the city of Hiroshima. I did not speak of my sorrow, as I was too appreciative of what my teacher had already done for me. I tried to think of ways to repay her in some form meaningful to her as a teacher.

I had thought that the very best gift would be to honor her mission. I informed Ms. Jones that I was willing to be baptized as a Christian. In the summer before Ms. Jones left the country, I accepted the sprinkling of water over my head, and heard a minister pronounce myself a disciple of a foreign-named son of God, Christ. It was an act of giving, rather than a conversion of my soul, for I did not know any better way of loving back someone who was leaving me again. My teacher was just as pleased and gratified as I had anticipated.

On the day of Ms. Jones's departure, I did not go inside the train station or see her. I stayed outside and watched the send-off party leave. No one saw me standing there. I was satisfied that at the end of her mission and a long "rainy day," my teacher was taking with her the story that I gave her as my farewell gift.

10

Road without Turning

Sitting on the front row for the Vespers service was not exactly the easiest thing for anyone, but I made a willing exception on one afternoon, in late November of my senior year. The student body was assembled in the chapel auditorium, waiting to hear from an "outstanding student leader" by the name of Dr. James H. Robinson of New York. He was representing the Board of Foreign Missions of the Presbyterian Church.

I craned my neck to see if the man on the poster had taken his seat on the stage. "An outstanding student leader," I repeated in my mind. "Yes, I need to hear him." I had been struggling with the question of effective leadership ever since I was elected to head the high school student body of over seven hundred. I was a natural at spotting issues that affected the students and that were important to them. Leading the council members in encouraging classmate participation was new territory for me.

I looked to Ms. Johnson, the assistant principal and the advisor to the council, as well as the most progressive faculty member, to lend a hand. She was delighted to give an orientation after listening

108

to my plea that we simply didn't know how to be leaders. It turned out that Ms. Johnson didn't quite know how to teach young Japanese girls to be leaders, either.

Her weekly seminars focused on parliamentary procedure in such microscopic detail that it put everyone to sleep. The girls who were eager to learn the "how to" of leading were prepared to tackle new concepts, but were really let down. A talk on Western parliamentary procedure missed the target entirely, but the girls got the message. If they wanted to get anything done, they had to find a way themselves. Whatever we needed to learn had to come from our own hands, since no one else wanted to take the risk of teaching us to become too unconventional. After that came a handful of major events organized by my cabinet and myself. On Culture Day, we organized magnificent displays, performances, and guest speakers that included the nation's minister of Culture and Education. How exhausting that time was, but fun, too!

The poster for the speaker showed a very different sort of individual from the usual evangelists. We were used to seeing fair-haired and sharp-featured individuals. Dr. Robinson, we were told, was a "Negro" gentleman. Only a few of us had been introduced to anything or anyone remotely connected with "Negro" people. This connection was made through Ms. Tarr, who taught English, sometimes using Negro Spirituals. The songs were hauntingly beautiful and poetic. She described these people as having had very difficult times which made them more spiritual. The girls learned to sing "Swing Lo Sweet Chariot," "Jacob's Ladder," and many other songs, clapping hands and harmonizing, soon forgetting all about the song's origins.

Turning around, I finally saw a man of stocky build, fast approaching from the side entrance. He was wearing a dark suit over a clerical collar and shirt, hurrying to take his seat on the stage. All eyes followed the gentleman visitor to take in every detail, for, we had never seen a speaker of his appearance before. There on the stage was a man with a skin color darker than anyone had seen before, with short curly hair, and glasses. There was a powerful personal presence about him, before he even uttered a word. His nose was broad, and his lips were thick, but it was his eyes that stood out even through his glasses. They were the most piercing and serious pair of eyes, conveying that someone extraordinary was behind them.

I remembered distinguished guests coming through my town before, like Helen Keller with Ms. Thompson, and even the Emperor of Japan. The man before us appeared to rank among the memorable.

Ms. Wilson, a tall, slender, and frail looking missionary who taught music opened the program by giving a brief introduction. Dr. James H. Robinson had a distinguished career as a community leader who inspired hundreds of Ivy League college students to help build summer camps for Harlem children in New Hampshire. He was a graduate of the Union Theological Seminary and Lincoln University. Coming from rural Tennessee and without any support from his family, he established a church and a thriving community center single-handedly. All of this information did not hold much meaning for me, as I had very little knowledge of American society until he began to talk about himself as a person.

After the customary salutations and mention of his understanding of the suffering of the people of Hiroshima, Dr. Robinson began to describe his own life experiences. As he talked, I was reminded of the story of *Uncle Tom's Cabin*, a book from my childhood library that I hadn't given any attention to since I was a small child.

He conjectured that the people of Hiroshima must have felt very discouraged, and he thought that there was a good reason to feel that way. He was truly sorry that we had to go through what we did. He pointed out that in the history of the human race, victimization has existed through the ages, and that one has the choice of either remaining a victim or going beyond it. He drew parallels between his life experiences and our current pain and sufferings. He suggested that to go beyond victimization we should identify with something much greater than ourselves.

We could see that being as dark skinned as he was, he could not escape the binds of his society. His boyhood was marred by the constant pull to the fields and away from schooling, so his father could have an extra hand. His mother died early, and his struggles to survive continued. Finally, he made it to the ministry. The entire account was impressive and profoundly moving. I was mesmerized, tears streaming down my face, without the aid of a handkerchief, for I had not expected to cry during this service. He said his life was a journey on the "Road without Turning."

The spellbinding speech had a most astonishing effect on my attitude. Here I thought we had no choice but to be victims, but there, beyond our life experiences were others who had overcome their victimization. Dr. Robinson invited those in Hiroshima who were oppressed by their experiences to rise above their suffering as he had. He spoke of a Christian God in this context. There was no self-righteous arrogance nor were there repetitious invitations to salvation. A warm and humble man was inviting us to take a "Road without Turning" along with him, away from vindication, self-pity, or a vast empty hole in which victims can so often find themselves engulfed. He was singling out only one name, "Christ," and one power, "love."

Listening to him was like being carried along on an ocean wave where the infinite possibility of going beyond the horizon existed. God and Christ were not spoken of as theological principles exported by devout believers from another land. The binding agent was love, love that never died throughout the millenniums of our history. I don't know how this began to register in my mind then. A mystic core of one's personal relationship to one's universe and its Maker was now inviting my attention. Perhaps it was because our speaker had come out of a humble origin. Perhaps it was because it was obvious that he knew the language of personal pain. Whatever it was that he came to share, we understood the message. We could dance again and sing praises to the life that we had come to detest earlier.

It was then that I remembered again the times in late December when my mother used to sing to me a Christmas carol, "Joy to the World." I remembered her speaking about attending a Sunday school in Tokyo out of curiosity. She followed a friend. She learned songs from a Catholic priest who was gentle and kind to the children. That was all she said about her experience. Every Christmas, however, gifts from Santa Claus arrived, even during the war. We sang our favorite carol with vigor. I had not thought of it since we had stopped celebrating Christmas after my mother was gone.

After the Vespers service, a smaller group of students gathered around Dr. Robinson for a question and answer session in the back of the auditorium. Taking a seat in the circle, I thanked him for his inspiring message on behalf of the student body. His genial ways with young people were apparent, and I decided to ask him something that had been on my mind.

I asked him, "If a student was interested in working with social problems and studying Christianity, should she attend college and study social problems, or should she study theology?" Listening carefully, his warm eyes went back to a piercing stare, as he replied, "If I were you, I would come to the United States and study there." I laughed and told him that it would be out of the question to go so far away, and that it was not a realistic solution. He suggested that I not dismiss the idea too quickly and think it over.

We continued to ask questions about his student work and ideas on leadership training. He spoke about his community center in Harlem, New York, and the summer camps for the children from that area, built by student volunteers from colleges all over his country. He was able to reach out to others who dreamed with him. His appeal came from his strong belief that we were all connected in the brotherhood of the human race, beyond any divisions of race, creed, or social status. His actions came across as truly genuine. He appeared to be entirely comfortable now with a group of foreign students who barely spoke English. It was an awesome and inspiring experience to be in such a man's presence.

My head was spinning as I headed home. The content of his speech and his totally unworkable, but still provocative suggestions persisted. If Helen Keller were to inspire a young deaf-mute in another land, she would have done no better. The theme of an oppressed group rising above oppression stayed in my mind. I wondered if this was an individual exception or something "Negro" people, even young people as a whole, cultivated. I thought I could really benefit from learning about this kind of spirituality, as I was yet far from it myself.

In my subsequent contacts with Dr. Robinson, who stayed in the city for more engagements, I learned that there were Negro colleges that were considered outstanding, and that, he would be pleased to introduce me to a few of these schools. We exchanged correspondence in the months that followed, and an application to Bennett College in Greensboro, North Carolina, was processed with his recommendation.

I kept Papa updated on the situation, and he presented my interest in studying abroad to the family for their approval. He never once objected or questioned the wisdom of my plan, though there had never been anyone from our family who studied abroad before. The only recollection the family had about anyone in the family leaving for a foreign land was Grandma Tamano's brother, who emigrated to Brazil earlier in the century. The trouble with it was that he had not been heard from much, and they had no idea how things worked out for him. No one had any idea what it might be like for a young woman of my age to live in an American society, and to be in a "Negro" community. Neither did I. The college bulletin from Bennett was the sole source of our information; it contained pictures of a stunningly beautiful campus for my nervous relatives.

The last difficulty was funding this education, including the transportation to the United States. Papa's finances were far from prosperous, and the Japanese government was disallowing dollar transactions. Anyone heading for a U.S. institution had to depend on a sponsor who could underwrite the project.

With all of these complications, the planning came to a halt, but I continued to hope for a last minute miracle. I processed my visa for entry to the United States during the summer of 1952. In the meantime, I took an entrance exam to Jogakuin College, since there was no support from my family for a college outside of Hiroshima.

A classmate of mine, Yoshino, was also planning to study in the United States. She was headed for Ohio where her maternal aunt resided. Several Nisei students were returning to the United States, and the number of the United States–bound students was increasing.

An alarmed young missionary, knowing the level of her students' English ability, came to warn us that we would not be able to handle an American college education. She urged that our plan be postponed until after we finished college in Japan first.

The president of Jogakuin Consortium, Dr. Hirose, a Ph.D. from Columbia University, called me into her office and, based on her knowledge of American society and its educational institutions, urged me not to apply to a Negro college.

They might as well have saved their breath, for the determination of the students, with their respective plans in progress, was not about to be changed. Our English may have been grossly deficient, but we were well informed in our own language, and we were definitely not underachievers, which was something that was often misunderstood by foreigners.

In the spring of 1952, the yearly cherry blossom season came to pass when Jogakuin College, built on the side of a small mountain in Hiroshima, welcomed its new freshmen. I entered as an English major, because there were no other choices. I did not mind building language skills before leaving the country, but the time of my departure was yet unknown. I kept my still high hopes of leaving the country to myself.

Courses in English, philosophy, Latin, and music started out smoothly. The philosophy course would have been challenging, but it consisted mostly of note taking, as the teacher read from his own notes without a pause. It was an exercise in shorthand, rather than critical review or thinking, which I craved. The English class required the Oxford English Dictionary along with the text of Robert Louis Stevenson's *The Strange Case of Dr. Jekyll and Mr. Hyde*. Although I enjoyed the literary flavor, its prospective value in daily life abroad was very questionable.

In late Spring, Yoshino, my classmate, secured her cross-Pacific boat ticket, through the sponsorship of a Methodist Women's group, and was happily on her way to her Ohio relatives. The boat tickets were hard to come by and they had to be reserved months in advance, if not longer. I had no funds even in July or early August for such an expense.

Then came a series of totally unexpected events, late in August. I received a cable from Dr. Robinson, stating that money in the amount of $350 had been cabled to a Presbyterian representative in Tokyo towards my boat fare. I later learned that this money was collected from the congregation of his church in Harlem. A regular ticket reservation at this late date was not available until the following year.

In desperation I contacted a former president of Jogakuin Consortium, who was a graduate of the Union Theological Seminary of New York, and asked if he might have any connections to help me. He spoke with the party to whom the money was cabled, and together, they were able to book me a passage to America, due to a last minute cancellation of another passenger, on a freight ship named the *President McKinley*, due to set sail on September 6, 1952.

There was hardly time to bid farewell to anyone at the end of the summer vacation, or barely enough time to collect my belongings together to pack. Papa and I rushed around to a luggage store downtown and he bought me three small shiny suitcases to pack all my meager winter and summer clothes, plus books and a blanket. We sewed dollar bills totaling about $30 inside my suit jacket, as the Japanese were not allowed to take dollar currency outside the country, but I had to have some cash to travel with. My relatives who had not believed this feat of departure could be seriously attempted, much less accomplished, were stunned.

On September 4, 1952, the Hiroshima station platform saw a crowd of Tamura clans-people bidding farewell to a little girl, the likes of whom they had never seen, except for her mother once among them. Grandmother Tamano held onto my hand, saying she just couldn't let it go. She was afraid that she might never see me again if she did. It might have been that she was also remembering the time of farewell to her younger brother, who left Japan long ago.

He never returned, and they never heard about him. Testuko-san was holding my baby stepbrother in her arms, crying as she waved her good-bye. Papa and I rode on the train to Tokyo together.

Unlike Mama and I, Papa and I seldom chatted between ourselves since my childhood. I knew from his actions that he cared very much. He was always better in answering or responding to my questions and requests than initiating conversations. I had thought that was how all Japanese fathers acted.

But on this trip, he was busy initiating the coversation and giving instructions. He gave a list of all the addresses of the members of the Tamura families, close and distant, to whom expressions of appreciation should be sent, after I arrived at my destination. Papa even worried about how I might care for a cold or a stomachache while in the States.

He made sure I had a watch, picking up a little Seiko with a green band. Papa emptied his own black leather wallet and a small notebook size zip-case for me to take. Arriving after an overnight train ride in Tokyo, we spent the last night at a small inn, the stay arranged by his friend, Ryo-chan from Takashimaya, who was an executive by that time.

The ship, *President McKinley*, was to set sail exactly at 1:00 P.M. sharp the following day. My former president Rev. Dr. Matsumoto, and my father took me to the pier in Yokohama where the ship was docked. Many years later I saw Rev. Dr. Matsumoto and President Truman on TV in the United States, and I remembered his seeing me off for my journey to the United States.

It was an awesome sight to see a ship that was about to take me away from my country. Dr. Matsumoto accompanied me to my cabin, and introduced me to the captain of the ship, Mr. Robertson, a tall, friendly gentleman in a blue and white uniform with a handsome captain's hat. Dr. Matsumoto explained my young age and the purpose of my trip, asking the man to kindly look after me. "Of course," the captain replied, he was happy to accommodate the young student.

As the ship's heavy resounding whistle hauntingly cried out into the Yokohama sky, the moment I had waited for so eagerly arrived, yet it was strangely painful as well. As the hum of the whistle traveled through the air, I remembered thinking to myself, "I may never return, and if I ever do, it will never be the same." Dr. Matsumoto and Papa stood on the pier waving their hands, while the ship slowly gained its distance from the shore until their figures faded into a dim spot in the horizon. Papa remained there waving. I heard a man behind me nudging his wife, as he whispered, "Give her the binoculars, it's her father, let her see him one more time."

My two cabinmates were American wives of servicemen returning home. The accommodations were first class, the only class the freighter had. I was grateful we were not at the bottom of the ship, as we would have been the last to come out of the ship if it started to sink. The sailing time was usually four weeks or longer, including a stop at Hawaii, but this ship was making a direct crossing to San Francisco in less time. Classes at Bennett College had already started and I hoped the ship's schedule stayed on time.

The two women and I slept in a small cabin with a bed and a bunk bed, the wives on the bottom beds and I on the upper bunk. One was blond and the other brunette, as different as night and day. The blond lady, Sally, was gregarious, and loved visiting Captain Robertson, and when he was occupied, she visited with the ship's First Mate, John. Each night she came back to the cabin quite late. The other lady, Janet, did not approve of her roommate's conduct and socializing, making frequent remarks about it, intimating that she could do the same but was choosing not to do so because her husband would not want her to. I just listened, but I doubt Miss Sally did.

My first ordeal on the ship came shortly after the call for the first meal in the dining room. Unlike my earlier eating out ventures to noodle houses and cafes, where most restaurants had wax samples of the dishes on the menu, there was no hint of what type of food or drink each menu item referred to.

I was tongue-tied when a smiling uniformed waiter of chocolate-brown skin came to take my order. Perusing the menu quickly up and down, the only words of English that I recognized were, *peas, carrots,* and *potatoes* from Ms. Anderson's English class, where we read the *Tale of Peter Rabbit*. Nothing from Stevenson's *Dr. Jekyll and Mr. Hyde* was of use for deciphering the mystery in front of me. The waiter was a bit puzzled by my order of only vegetables, but soon returned with peas, carrots, and potatoes, all rather tasteless compared to the Japanese method of cooking in soup stocks and sauces, in which no vegetables ever tasted this bland. I had to drink a lot of water to wash them down, while other guests dined on an assortment of savory, aromatic, and delicious foods.

This was a lesson not to be repeated, I decided. I took my pocket dictionary with me to the empty dining room before the next bell and carefully studied the content of the next menu. I still didn't know what most of the food looked or tasted like, so the simple solution was just to look around and discreetly request the same dish. Soon I was eating like a connoisseur.

During the long voyage, the nine or ten passengers became well acquainted. I spent a lot of time with a sixteen-year-old Philippino girl traveling with her family to America. They were moving to the States for a new life. We talked about our lives, hopes, and dreams. The older couple with the binoculars were White Russians who had lived in Japan for some time, but were retiring to the United States. Janet was going home to her folks in the South, and Sally's husband, a military doctor, was waiting for her somewhere in the East.

My favorite activity by far was to go up on the deck and walk to the rear of the ship, watching the crushing ocean waves being left behind. There was nothing to see but the vast blue sky and the ocean itself; no island, no shores, but the character of the scenery changed with the wind and the changing clouds. Three times it changed drastically.

We were awakened late in the middle of one night by sudden movements of the ship, going up and down and side to side. Janet found herself thrown out of the bed to the floor. Sally was still away visiting. My body was stopped from hitting the floor by a wood rail, placed there just for that reason. The captain informed us that we were in a typhoon. It raged for days. Dishes were breaking, and fewer and fewer people showed up for their meals.

My Philippino friend and the rest of the passengers were sick during the entire storm. Even the thought of food made them sick. So long as the ship kept afloat, however, the motion of the ship did not bother me. I was one of the very few passengers who didn't miss a meal. I was happy that the ship was sailing even faster because of the wind beneath it. I hummed the song of the divine wind that rescued the port of Hakata under attack by the Mongol forces of tens of thousands many centuries ago. No one even noticed.

After the winds subsided, the ship continued to sail uneventfully in the hands of the able Captain Robertson until one morning when I saw the most moving sight of my life. The Golden Gate Bridge of San Francisco came into view. All my dreams, all my pain, and all my searches were about to meet together guiding my uncertain future into a yet unseen land.

An intense anticipation and rush of energy filled my body from head to toe. There was nothing tangible that I had touched or seen in America as of yet. My books about Tom Sawyer and Huck Finn, my mother's *Gone with the Wind,* and Lincoln's humble beginning in my illustrated books, were far from the scenic view of the city in the bay the ship was now entering. The modern buildings clustered like an island mound, coming closer and closer as they finally neared the dock in San Francisco.

In my excitement, I assumed that we would be getting off the ship right away. As it turned out, we had to wait for many hours before we could touch the land. The first "American" resident was in my view from the ship as I came out to the deck early in the morning to watch the shore. A middle-aged, short, disheveled-looking lady wearing bright lipstick, was leaning over a wire fence, looking at the ship as if waking up with a big hangover. She wore a mismatched pair of socks with a red sock on one foot and yellow sock on the other. My introduction to America was swiftly beginning.

More hours were spent waiting for the customs officials to inspect our papers and belongings. I was dressed in my best clothes for the occasion: a black felt hat, elastic tied so it would not be blown away, and a brown suit from the used clothing chest that was sent from the kind women of the Methodist Church in the States.

The suit was a couple of sizes too large and had been taken in to fit. I wore my best socks with yellow and brown stripes, and a pair of brown shoes to match. The shoes were a bit tight on my feet, but I hoped they would fit in time. I walked down the moving steps as proudly as could be, believing my appearance was near perfection.

The customs inspector was less impressed and a bit gruff. On the concrete pavement of the pier were a few plain tables where he sat. The contents of my suitcases were emptied and shuffled around, coming apart after my very careful repacking from the night before. Before I could tell him to stop shaking, the sound of falling and rolling objects caught every one's ears to the consternation of the inspector.

"Wait sir, I am losing my marbles," I hollered, running after little glass balls that Cousin Hideyuki had given me a long time ago. They had been left in the temple to which I had been evacuated. I retrieved them long after the war ended. They were the only keepsakes I had of my cousin.

"You are losing your what?" The inspector could not believe what he was seeing and hearing. The people around him were trying very hard not to laugh at this point. I explained to him in great embarrassment, still collecting the pieces, and running in every direction, that these were irreplaceable keepsakes from someone dear who had died. His gruff demeanor softened and relaxed somewhat, as he allowed my marbles to come into the country.

Thus my journey on the road without turning began.

11

America, America

Journey to the South

Though the beautiful vision of the Golden Gate Bridge was fresh in my mind, I headed for Bennett College in a state of shock. The country I had never set my feet or eyes upon was finally here. After three typhoons and thirteen days on a sailing ship, walking on the concrete pavement felt a bit strange at first. The people around me were actually the very same folks I was taught were our mortal enemies ready to exterminate us, and vice versa. The people on the streets gave no hint of a capability for beastliness as they went on about their business. They just looked different. Even the Oriental faces appeared foreign. They did not even look like the Chinese and Korean folks at home. These were Americans. American soil and American air probably changed them, I thought. Would it happen to me? I wondered.

One of the suitcases had already popped at the hinges when the immigration inspector hurridly tried to stuff my belongings back into it. I had a dismal vision of having to carry a bag over my shoulder like Santa Claus all the way to North Carolina. Luckily, the broken luggage was repaired by a retired missionary to China, Dr. White, who had been contacted by Rev. Robinson to meet me at the pier. Rev. Robinson had forwarded to Dr. White my train fare to Bennett, which had been raised by the congregation of his Harlem church.

The day was filled with anticipation for the new adventure about to begin. Filled with a youthful and totally uninformed vision of America, I trotted in small quick steps trying to keep up with the tall white-haired man with long strides. "Right off the boat" probably described even my outfit consisting of an altered brown suit from the missionaries' give-away closet, a black felt hat, and striped socks. I might have stumbled here and there as my tight brown shoes pinched my toes.

Before leaving the pier, we were met by another welcoming party, Ms. Merrell of the Methodist Missions. She had been contacted by Ms. Jones from the Hiroshima Mission School. She was relieved to see that Dr. White had already taken care of my arrival. She also insisted that I stop by the "Mexican Block" near the Los Angeles station at the next stop. Without having any idea what the Mexican Block was all about, I promised her I would.

My first American meal was a supper in a crowded place Dr. White called a "cafeteria." His Chinese students favored the place because one could choose whatever item seemed appealing. They loved jello and rolls with butter, he said, pointing to them on his tray. "When in Rome, do as the Romans do," or "just follow the elders' examples" came to me quickly. My Chinese counterparts must have been taught the same.

Dr. White also took me to a "drugstore" which he thought was a typically American place to visit. Contrary to its name, the "drugstore" turned out to be like a general store with a little of everything. My fashion statement, or perhaps the fact that I was accompanied by a tall white-haired gentleman, was apparently sensational. Never in my life in Japan had I been so stared at as I shopped.

Clutching my train tickets purchased with the money Dr. Robinson had forwarded, I boarded the train and began my long journey across America. I knew it was to be the start of a lifelong journey. An endless story began that day. The immediate destination, I reminded myself, was the "Mexican Block."

It was near dusk, my favorite time, by the time the train pulled into Los Angeles station. As soon as someone pointed out the direction in which the "Mexican Block" was located, I headed outside the station hastily, thinking I could be back before dark. I was trying to make out the streets ahead when a shadow suddenly came up to my side.

"Hey, Lady, where you headed to? Can I help you?"

"Thank you, but no, I'm headed to the Mexican Block," I said, nervously. In the light he was a young man of golden complexion and a lean build with black wavy hair, standing with an open smile. My negative reply did not stop him from walking right along by my side. I didn't even know where I was when he grabbed my arm and began to lead me towards the busy streets ahead. I was too petrified to scream or run, but judging from the non-English sounds I began to hear and the Latin features of the crowd, we apparently had arrived at the "Mexican Block" by this time.

I was tongue-tied. Just as in the age-old expression, I could not believe this was happening to me. Having just gotten here, I already seemed to be in some sort of captivity. I couldn't think of any situation like this in my or anyone else's experiences. Where I came from, no men and women mixed without an introduction.

Trying to look unafraid, I decided to pay closer attention to the shop displays. I had no idea what Mama might have done or Papa might have said. They most surely would not have liked it if I disappeared into thin air. Now I was in the middle of a crowded market that I didn't even know how I had gotten to, and I had no way of predicting how the "captivity" was going to end. Just then, I saw a portrait artist working on a pad. As I leaned over to look at it, my young captor whispered something to the artist. I became the artist's instant subject. In a few minutes a caricature portrait was ready, complete with a black hat and a cupid in the upper corner.

The Mexican Block came to an end abruptly as we reached a stone building with blinking rooftop neon sign ". . . Bar . . ." The young man pointed to the stone steps leading to a cellar below, the whole setting looking like a Casbah scene from French movies I used to see in Hiroshima. This was it. I had to do something instantly. I hadn't been taught to scream, but my leg muscles had the super training from my Seibi Academy days some years ago.

I vaulted into the dark with the rolled up portrait under my arm, but I had no idea if I was running in the right direction until the lights of the station came into my view. The sight of the ladies' room was never so welcomed as that night. I stayed there for the rest of the evening until my train's departure.

In retrospect the whole ordeal was probably an innocent encounter with a young Latino lad who was being hospitable to a student visitor as she wandered into his territory at dusk. When I think of the stone stairway into which I was nudged to descend that night, however, I still feel a tinge of cold sweat after all these years.

I awoke safe and sound the next morning on the train. We were moving eastward across the southern half of the American continent. The dry flat land stretched from one horizon to the other.

"Where are we?" I wondered out loud.

"Texas, honey," a sweet nasal reply came back.

So this is Texas that we heard so much about. It was stupendous to see the sun rise and set behind a horizon instead of disappearing behind mountain ranges. After I overheard a woman passenger raving about her hometown of San Antonio, I followed behind her when she got off, just to taste the air. The blazing heat was nearly suffocating. It was like an oven. American people must really like it hot. I remembered how the missionaries used to wonder how we could stand to take such hot baths or drink beverages so hot. Being able to live in heat like this and even enjoy it was even more amazing.

By the time the train reached New Orleans, I had a handful of newsy postcards to mail. Without even thinking that it might have been another color here, I looked all around for a red mail box as I had been accustomed to in Japan. I almost put my cards in a trash can. Afterwards I was told the color was green. I would never have known the cards didn't reach anybody.

Newlyweds.
*Hideko's parents,
Jiro and Kimiko
Tamura, in
Tokyo, 1933.*

A Happy Beginning. *Hideko with her mother, 1934.*

First Studio Portrait. *Hideko at age 2, looking a bit unsettled by the studio camera and flash.*

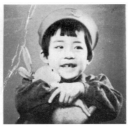

Full of Mischief. *Portrait of Hideko at age 4, taken at Mitsukoshi Department Store.*

A Rest from Play. *Hideko and her mother, Tokyo, 1937, in a garden where they had been playing on rocks near a stone lantern.*

Mother and Daughter. *Hideko with her mother by the gate of their house in Tokyo, 1937.*

Waiting to Join the Tamura Household. *Hideko and her mother on a sun deck at the Niitani family's home, shortly after their arrival in Hiroshima, winter 1938. Hideko's cousins Hiroshi and Shoji are also pictured.*

Changing World. *The first mother-daughter portrait of Hideko and her mother taken by the Tamura family photographer, winter 1938. This was taken soon after Hideko and her parents had moved to the Tamura estate in Hiroshima after they were accepted back into the Tamura clan. Hideko is 4¹/2 years old.*

An
Introduction
to Buddhist
Rites.
*Hideko
upon her
initiation at
the Tokuoji
Temple in
Hiroshima,
winter1939.*

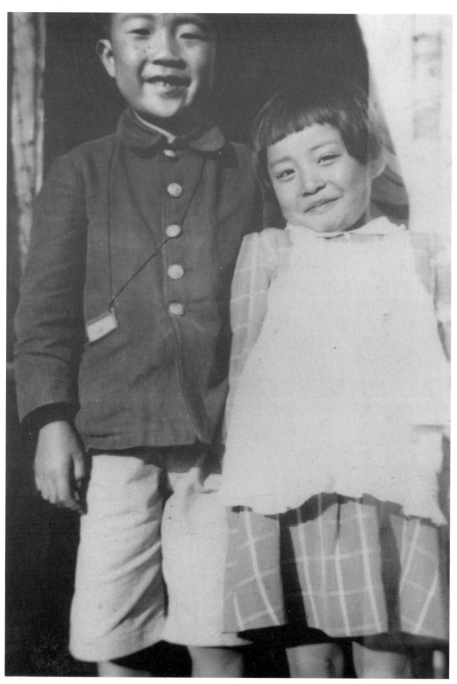

Chums Right from the Start. *Cousin Hideyuki and Hideko, aged 7 and 5, respectively, spring 1939.*

Send-off for a Soldier:
The Tamura clan gathered to honor Hideko's father, Jiro, before he was sent to China, 1938. Front row from right: Cousin Keiju, Cousin Hideyuki, Grandfather Hidetaro, Hideko's father (Jiro), Grandmother Tamano, Hideko, Aunt Chitose, Cousin Mitsuo, Aunt Fumiko, Uncle Hisao. Back row from right: Cousin Shoji, Aunt Yoshiko and her husband (a fourteenth generation heir to a Japanese inn on Shikoku Island patronized by the Emperor and his family), Cousin Hiroshi, Uncle Tokuichi, Hideko's mother (Kimiko), Aunt Shizuko and her husband, Aunt Kiyoko.

School at Last. *Hideko as a first-grader at Seibi Academy, April 1940.*

Jiro Tamura. *Hideko's father, a man with artistic aspirations, was working as a Nissan salesman to support his family when he was served his draft notice, the dreaded "red paper." He became a soldier for the Imperial Army in 1938.*

Kimiko Tamura. *Hideko's mother during World War II in Hiroshima, just before her husband was sent on a wartime mission, winter 1942.*

World War II Family Portrait. *This photograph was taken on the eve of Captain Tamura's mission to Hong Kong. He was not expected to return. Front row from right: Grandfather Hidetaro, Hideko's father (Captain Jiro Tamura), Hideko, Hideko's mother (Kimiko). Back row from right: Uncle Hisao, Cousin Hideyuki, Grandmother Tamano, Aunt Yoshiko, Aunt Kiyoko. Not pictured is Aunt Fumiko who was confined to bed with pregnancy complications while carrying Cousin Kumiko, 1942.*

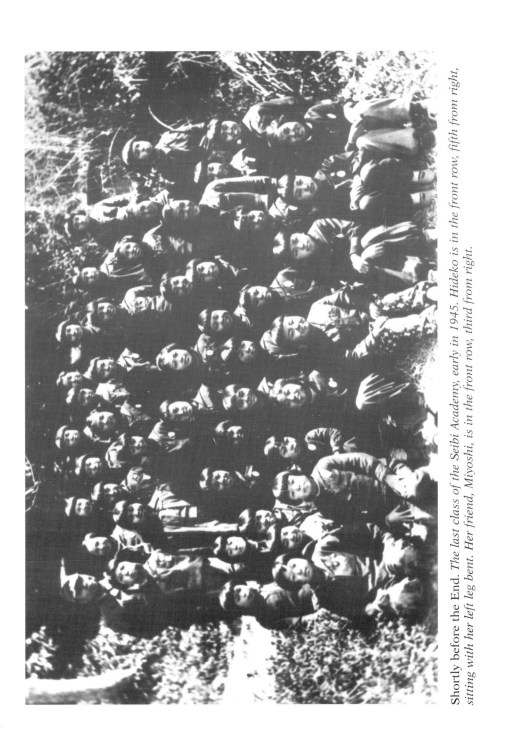

Shortly before the End. *The last class of the Seibi Academy, early in 1945. Hideko is in the front row, fifth from right, sitting with her left leg bent. Her friend, Miyoshi, is in the front row, third from right.*

The Death of Hiroshima. *The atomic bomb was dropped on Hiroshima on August 6, 1945. The steel frame of the Sun Movie Theater, located 850 meters from the epicenter, bent like melted candy in the thermal wind.*

After the Bomb. *This is one of many scenes of devastation that greeted Hideko and other survivors when they returned to Hiroshima after the bomb and the raging fires had destroyed the city. The structure in the foreground used to be a Methodist church. One of the structures in the background used to be the Fukuya Department Store. Another one of the tall building in the background was where the Chugoku Newspaper, read all over the middle region of Japan, had been published.*

Downtown Hiroshima after the Bomb. This picture was taken facing south, with the financial district and the mountain, Hijiyama, in the left background. Ujina Harbor, where Hideko's father worked, is in the far right background. The epicenter of the bomb was Shima Hospital, which was located (in approximately the center of the upper left quadrant) along the road leading to the Ota River. The large building in the right foreground has been left standing to this day and is now known as the Memorial Dome. Seibi Academy, where Hideko attended school, was located in the foreground to the left, just outside the frame of this photograph. It was leveled by the bomb.

More Damage from the Thermal Wind. *This photograph of homes located 2 kilometers south of the epicenter in Hiroshima was taken between August 10 and 12, 1945.*

The Scene in Hiroshima 1.5 Kilometers West of the Epicenter. *This photograph was taken in August 1945. (The preceding five photographs of Hiroshima are reprinted from* **The Archival Records of the Damage from the A-Bomb in Hiroshima,** *vol. 1, edited and published by The City Office of Hiroshima, Hiroshima, Japan, 1971.)*

Lost in the Country. *After the bomb was dropped, Hideko lived out in a rural area and attended Kabe Girls' School. Here she is as a seventh-grader in 1946. Notice that her tag is only pinned on. If her mother had been alive, no doubt it would have been sewn on properly.*

The Magic of
Imagination.
*Hideko attempted to
bring to life stories
from her childhood.
Here she is as the
Frog Prince from*
**The Frog and the
Princess,** *1947.*

The Cast of **The Frog and the Princess.** *Hideko helped her classmates
put on this play at Kabe Girls' School in 1947. She scripted it, designed
the stage sets, and found the costumes. Hideko is pictured front right.*

Friendly Cousins. *Hideko with her cousin, Kumiko, Hideyuki's sister, spring 1948. Hideko's clothes are her own mother's hand-me-downs. The outfit had been given to her mother's younger sister and was later passed on to Hideko.*

A Lasting Friendship. *Hideko with her friend, Etsuko, summer 1951. Hideko is wearing an outfit from a missionary's donation closet while Etsuko is wearing a new dress made by her mother's seamstress. Today Etsuko is a freelance journalist.*

Hideko and Classmates. *Hiroshima Jogakuin students in their school uniforms, spring 1951. Hideko (back row second from left) and Yoshino (back row far right) came to the U.S. to attend college. The other girls shown here all went on to have successful professional careers (as educators, writers, or media personalities), though this was not typical for Japanese women at the time.*

Do you have something for an empty heart? *This is the missionary who did. Hideko with Ms. Jones, a Methodist missionary from Odessa, New York, 1950.*

By the Ota River. *Hideko in the place where she found solace watching the sunset and the flowing water, where the railroad grass (clearly visible in the background) grew and where she found four-leaf clovers by the hundreds. Summer 1952.*

Wondering if the Past Can Be Left Behind. *Hideko, visiting the rubble of the Memorial Dome in Hiroshima shortly before leaving for the United States, August 1952. She is wearing a new outfit made by her stepmother, copied from* **Seventeen** *magazine. Hideko's stepmother was very helpful when it came to preparing Hideko for her departure.*

Touching the Memorial Dome One Last Time. *Hideko, in August 1952, when people were still permitted to walk among the ruined structure and sketch, touch, or contemplate the steel and concrete.*

Homage and Farewell. *Hideko visiting the Peace Memorial for the victims of the atomic bomb. The names of Kimiko (her mother), Miyoshi (her friend), Cousins Hideyuki, Kiyotsune, Tomoko, and countless others are recorded in the sepulcher.*

America, at Last. *After three typhoons and endless waves, Hideko found the Golden Gate Bridge in San Francisco Bay to be a very welcome sight, September 1952.*

Books and More Books. *Hideko at Bennett College in Greensboro, North Carolina, in October 1952, after a cross-country rail trip filled with surprises.*

Christmas in Pennsylvania. *William and Ann Larson with son Eric opened their home to Hideko as her American family, December 1953.*

A Helpful Mentor. *Dr. James H. Robinson (standing next to Hideko) flanked by students whom he aided: Barbara Skaif from Iowa, Karioki Njuri from Kenya, and Hideko from Japan, summer 1954. Njuri, the son of a tribal chieftain, would later serve in the Kenyan legislature.*

Hideko's Father Visiting the U.S. *Hideko chatting with her father on Michigan Avenue in Chicago, October 1968. The occasion was Hideko's wedding.*

An Old Friend Revisited. *Hideko and retired missionary Ms. Jones, 1993.*

Takada from Kimita Village. *Takada was the village boy who did not taunt Hideko when she was feeling devastated and homesick during the evacuation to the rural village. Though she visited him much later, this is a high school picture from 1949.*

By the Sunny Inland Seashore. *Hideko, Aunt Fumiko, and Cousin Kumiko at the award-winning nursing home owned and managed by Cousin Kumiko, 1982. The nursing home, in Hiroshima Province, has been recognized for the innovative services it offers.*

New Family. *Hideko is flanked by her daughter, Miko, her son, Joshua, and her fiance, Robert, following her daughter's graduation from Wellesley College, June 2, 1995.*

On Another Sunny Day. *Thirty-two years after their original engagement, Hideko and Robert were married, in Wellesley Chapel, June 3, 1995.*

The long ride through Texas to New Orleans also gave me time to calm down a bit and get a feel for the country which obviously was quite different from the country I had just left. A short walk from the New Orleans station confirmed that even the great Mississippi River that I'd read about in *The Adventures of Tom Sawyer* and *Huckleberry Finn* was nothing like I had pictured in my mind. The rivers I had known were like the Ota River, clean and clear. In those rivers we could see the fish and shrimp darting from under the rocks on the river bed. This river had muddy water from shore to shore, the color resembling flooding rivers which I had seen from time to time back home.

When I returned to the station, I saw something that I had not noticed before. On the outside of the waiting room, there were signs marked WHITES ONLY on one and on the other, COLORED. I had no idea just what the COLORED meant other than something being coated with paint.

Peeking in I saw people of varying shades of brown skin in the Colored room. The "Color" apparently referred to one's skin coloring. I had grown up with a notion that being fair was something coveted for women but other than using powders and a sun umbrella I had not known there were specific consequences to a person's "Color" status. Now that I became aware of the signs, my immediate concern was deciding which of the two was my own entrance. I had never considered myself fair in spite of the characters of my name, which means "fair maiden." Actually, there weren't many I would have called so fair even among the women in my own family. So I stood outside as long as I could until the call of nature no longer could be resisted.

The question was the same for the other facilities as it was for the bathrooms. Shortly after noticing the first few, I realized the signs were everywhere. I didn't seem to belong to either group so I would use either facility, feeling very self conscious that I might be stopped at any moment and questioned about my presence. This notion was not conducive to a relaxed daily plumbing routine. No one stopped me, however, and I soon discovered the WHITES ONLY bathrooms were nicer and better-kept facilities.

Back aboard the train the divided sections were pretty well maintained for passenger seating all the way to Greensboro. The brown-skinned and fair-skinned passengers sat separately and remained apart at all times.

A vague connection then began to form in my mind about a group of Japanese who were treated differently, called *Buraku-min,* (a tribal people). Often, other Japanese avoided mention of the *Buraku* as if they did not exist. Both children and adults spoke in a hushed tone of voice when they spoke of *Buraku,* as if referring to a secret threat or intimidation. Neither of my parents ever behaved in this fashion so I knew nothing about the *Buraku* until I was in my teens. I remember asking my aunt one day what was so bad about coming in contact with them. She paused, looking almost afraid. She then whispered that I probably should say as little about the *Buraku* as possible. The description given to the *Buraku* origin was that they were animal handlers for many centuries and were considered impure among the non–animal eating population. Even after meat became a common and desirable part of our diet, the connotation of "uncleanliness" ascribed to the *Buraku* did not disappear.

There were no ostensible signs as to where one should sit or eat in Hiroshima, but there was a section of town called *Fukushima-cho* that no one I knew lived in or went near. It had not occurred to me until I saw the signs for the WHITES ONLY and the COLORED, that perhaps a similar sort of segregation had existed close to my home. Our segregation was on the basis of religion, or occupation, or perhaps simply by misfortune. I then recalled one theory that the *Burakus* were the descendants of the *Heike* clan who perished after it lost battles against the *Genji* in the late twelfth century. The descendants of the hunted men and their families had no means of survival except to kill animals and live a wayfarers' lot, so said a magazine article I read. The fallen outcast could have come from any failed group. The question of "color" and the safety of belonging to a majority seemed complicated everywhere.

Segregation notwithstanding, there were definitely homespun

hospitalities along the way. Back in occupied Japan, speaking with the soldiers was an unspoken taboo; here it was often the uniformed servicemen who helped carry my suitcases and hoisted the luggage in and out of the overhead compartments when the redcaps were nowhere to be found. It was not long ago that we had been told that we should take our own lives before letting the conquering American soldiers harm us. Thus coming in direct contact with the uniformed men for the first time was a bit scary. I was warmed, however, to discover that the readiness to lend a hand without expecting a favor in return seemed to be a common American practice.

Then, there was Mr. Redman, an elderly gentleman who liked to talk. He said he was blind in one eye and beginning to lose sight in the other. This did not seem to slow him down, however, as he moved about freely with surprising ease. As soon as he found out I was a foreign student, he insisted on a lunch treat in the dining car. He offered a lively description of typical American favorites.

"This is hamburger. You put the ketchup on and eat it like this."

After the meal, he grabbed a handful of sugar packets on the table and placed them in my hand.

"Here, take them, they're free."

"What if others after us need them?"

"Oh, they have plenty of it left." He was not concerned.

"I never took anything before."

"You didn't take them, *I* gave them to you." I was speechless.

Before getting off, Mr. Redman pulled out a five dollar bill from his wallet. He pushed it into my hand the same way he had done with the sugar packets.

"Here get yourself a treat on me or keep it for spending money, and good luck to you."

Shortly after my arrival on the Bennett campus, I wrote a thank you note to Mr. and Mrs. Redman at the address on his business card. I received a reply I had not expected. Along with a box of candy, there was a note from Mrs. Redman that her husband had passed away, but that he had told her about a student he had met on the train home on his last trip. By the time the train finally reached Greensboro, I had gotten to know things about America that no travel guide could have prepared me for.

I arrived at the Bennett campus about a month behind schedule. The girls found me a genial novelty, though there was a small number of foreign students already living in their midst, including a student from Japan. Shoko, my Japanese counterpart, and I quickly bonded together in spite of our very different personalities. They say that the first year in a foreign country is the hardest. Shoko, from Yamaguchi Province by the Sea of Japan, was a source of great comfort in my first, struggling year at Bennett. We probably would not have been so close, or found so much in common, had we met in Japan. Shoko was a poised and even-tempered "model student" as my teachers would have definitely called her back in Japan. She had taught Sunday school many years in her home church. As a rule, I stayed far away from such "saintly" colleagues, being averse to a comparison by others or even within myself. Our differences, however, were set aside temporarily as we extended support to each other. I don't know how either of us would have made it without the consoling presence of the other. We would sit and talk for hours over a cup of tea or share gifts of food sent from Japan.

Her reverent attitude towards her parents and home church used to inspire my own letter-writing home. Her manner of greeting her parents in her letters was nothing like "Dear Mama" or "Dear Papa," but rather something like "Revered Dear Mother Superior." I promptly imitated it in writing to my stepmother, and continued to use the same salutation ever after. It was marvelous to be able to relax speaking in Japanese in the privacy of a fellow Japanese. We recited and sang many songs together, even wartime melodies. Her favorite was one about the paratroopers jumping out in the sky. The words were incidental but the melodies we grew up with took us back to our lives during the wartime that neither of us had forgotten. We affirmed each other's well-being sometimes just by cooking a Japanese noodle dish in our room.

Pei Lee and Lillian made up the other half of the foreign students' circle. Coming from Mainland China via Formosa, they spoke fluent Chinese. I used to humor them by writing down Chinese characters as I sought common ground. The history of Sino-Japanese conflicts or any misery their families might have suffered from the Japanese expansion into their world could not be detected in their friendly demeanor towards Shoko and me. I hesitated to mention my father's love of Northern China which developed from being stationed there as an Imperial Army soldier or my grandfather's respect for his Chinese trading partner. I was afraid I might be reminding them of a hurtful past in ways I could not know.

They, too, were as different in temperament and interests as Shoko and I were. Pei Lee was a pleasingly plump science major. She had a corner room on the first floor in my dormitory and was always buried in books whenever I stopped by. Lillian was a tall and slender woman who expressed her feelings more readily than Pei Lee. When the slits in their Chinese dresses and their shapely thighs became the subject of campus conversation, the girls closed the open seams considerably lower. Sensuous effects were the farthest thing from their minds. They were hardly interested in any mixed socializing. Even Pei Lee with her very benign temperament seemed baffled by the controversy the "Chinese slits" caused. Lillian practically declared war on any suggestion about the height of her slit dress. The compromise I observed a short time later, however, was Lillian wearing an American black taffeta dress, standing regal and erect as she filled an usher's role in the chapel.

When we congregated, the four of us commented on these incidents freely, and compared our apprehensions about the American differences. We were probably trying to preserve our own identities by resisting outside influences.

Understanding my American colleagues took a different kind of acuity, one that I had not been quite prepared for. The sound of the speech I heard was quite unlike the English my missionary teachers had spoken. Our teachers' English had a lower pitch and their words were clearly enunciated for our benefit. Not only did I miss hearing the words altogether, once they were repeated I failed to understand the content. The dictionaries offered little aid. I remember a particularly confusing exchange that took place during my attempt to find the library. My friendly neighbor, Christine, pointed to the direction of the building and offered to walk with me, but she had to take care of a minor detail first. She asked me to give her a few minutes. But it was her next brief sentence that caused immediate confusion.

"Wait on me, hear?" she said.

I understood this to mean that she would carry me on her back but I was also to stay on that very spot, "here." After much confusion and a span of about a year, my ears became trained enough to the colloquialisms for me to hear and speak the new language almost like the natives. I remember the surprised expressions on the faces of my Eastern or Midwestern associates when they heard my *you-alls* and *hears*.

Beyond my linguistic trepidations, I was eager to learn about the thoughts and feelings of the young women living in my dormitory. The students came from all corners of the South and other parts of the country. Many came from quite well-heeled families judging from their possessions and their spending habits. There was something of an esprit de corps when small groups of women congregated just talking. These gatherings often took place over cold fried chicken brought back from home. All we had to hear was, "Uhum, it's chicken, you-all," and we were there.

My perennial why questions were tackled in good humor. It was here at Bennett that I learned that a number of the blue-eyed, blond-haired and very Caucasian-appearing students were also considered "colored." Somewhere in their background was a mixture of races and that took care of the label. In unrestrained conversations in the dorm rooms the women expressed the troubled feelings about the boundaries that kept their worlds apart. The hurt and anger lived side by side. These feelings were well-guarded and tucked away inside. I realized only years later that I had been privy to a genuine sharing of pain and joy among these women in those days.

On the lighter side, Clementine across the hallway taught me the art of lightening-up, with a myriad of funny high school stories and hair management ordeals. I came to appreciate the burden of hair management by watching the cumbersome process of straightening the hair and curling it again. The labels of *good* or *bad hair* were understandable in terms of the efforts required to achieve the desired end. It was ironic that many straight-haired women such as the Japanese frizzled their hair by perming.

Clementine and others introduced me to chips and soda to which I quickly formed fond relations, as well as the nickel-a-scoop ice cream cones of many varieties. My idea of happiness was the scent of strawberry traveling up my nostrils and strawberry ice cream melting on my tongue. Without a cash-paying job I was always strapped for money, but if anyone offered me a treat, strawberry ice cream was the one most desired.

Clementine's roommate, Christine, was a serious student with a penchant for buying new things downtown. She was also a very generous young woman, I found out. When I was beside myself one afternoon after my wallet was lost, Christine raised $8 in the dorm, actually a donation mostly from her spending allowance. She knew that I was saving from my meager cash to send a package to Hiroshima.

My roommate, Della, was from Baltimore. She comes closest to my vision of an all-American girl—bright, decent, and energetic. She was open and friendly without being intrusive. Her quick smiles brightened our room even on cloudy days. I am sure she knew little about my culture or of the details of my life experiences. She simply called me "roomy" and took me in like a next door chum. She gave me as much space or help as I needed. I don't know if I could have done the same were the situation reversed. Her ready attention and cheerful outlook were just what any newcomer needed, regardless of origin. I always felt better coming back to Della. Only twice did I see her slightly rattled in the entire two years I roomed with her. The first time was when the dorm matron gave us a checkmark for room inspection because I had forgotten to clear my bed before running to my early class. Upon my return,

Clementine warned me I was walking into bit of trouble. When I caught up with Della, she announced with clarity, so there would be no second occurrence.

"Roommate, you've got to hang up your coat and get your stuff off your bed."

"Yes, Della, I'm so sorry, I didn't know that was going to count against us," I apologized.

"Honey, just remember it the next time"

The other episode was not of my doing. It was more or less providential, and it rattled us both. One early morning before dawn, Della and I were awakened by a thunderous noise. It sounded as if the ceiling had come down. I screamed out to Della that the roof was falling. She did not believe me until we turned the lights on to see what had happened. On the floor between our beds was indeed a pile of large pieces of white clay that had fallen from the ceiling. I burst out laughing, proving myself right. Somehow it struck me funny that a small portion of our dorm ceiling would fall down in a beautiful American college dorm. It was not funny to Della at all.

"Roommate, this isn't funny at all, honey. We could'a been killed. Why they just missed us by just this much."

Later that day I heard her speaking very sternly to the dorm matron about our near-miss ordeal. She was upset. The difference between us, however, was that Della slept soundly from then on, but I didn't. I kept on waking up, fearing the next cave-in.

Despite my general progress in colloquial English, taking on the challenge of study in the new language turned out to be quite a daunting task. Back in the mission school I had left behind, I was accustomed to the comfort of being ahead without a great deal of effort. Students in Japanese colleges took laborious notes, but often that was the extent of the academic demands. Bennett demanded much more.

For the first time I was faced with more pages of material to read than I was able to keep up with. There were also term papers to write for every class. Writing used to be a breeze for me. I loved literature, and words came easily in my own language. It was an entirely different matter to think in one language and to express the same thoughts in another. I used to sit and stare into space searching for English words but only drawing a blank. I also realized I was missing more than half of the contents of the lectures. It took me hours to read a few pages in English while I could glance across a page written in Japanese and absorb almost all of the content.

Working in the library twenty hours a week left me even less time for my studies. I was clearly not up to the task before me but loath to accept defeat, I decided to give it a last ditch effort. I needed a place to study after the mandatory lights-out at 10:00 P.M. The only lighted place during the night was the bathroom on each floor. So on many occasions I snuck out to sit on the toilet seat, reading the assigned pages and composing my papers. From the bathroom window I watched the dark hours of night turn to the light of dawn. Often the work was still unfinished.

Eventually, a worried dorm-mate snitched on my nightly prowess. The dorm matron, Ms. Grier, swung open the door one night. I was crouched in the tub with a pillow on my back, wishing to shrink to a pinpoint. She ordered me back to my bed immediately.

"For heavens sake, Decco," she addressed me, "what in the world are you doing here at this time of the night?" She spoke in semi-disbelief.

"You'll make yourself sick, child. Go back to your room right now."

"But Ms. Grier, I still haven't finished my homework."

"Well, you'll just have to do it tomorrow. Maybe I'll get someone to help you."

Ms. Grier gave me a desk in the drawing room next to her quarters. She even asked another student to help with the class notes. My worry over depriving another student of her sleep was met with a chuckle from Ms. Grier.

"Honey, she's plenty healthy already."

My classmate was a tall husky woman nearly six feet tall.

After my problem was discovered in the dorm, I was able to discuss the problems with the faculty. Being quite sympathetic, they did not question my efforts or intellectual ability, understanding that the language switch for a young adult was a serious mechanical barrier. I was therefore granted extra time to finish papers and exams. I was grateful for being able to keep my dignity as a studious thinking human being. That was all I needed. At the end of that semester the report card listed A's in all subjects except for a PE class that featured folk dancing and line dancing (though I did learn to polka).

The supportive environment eased what might have been a chaotic year as I moved into the new routines. In those early years I was homesick not so much for Hiroshima but for the Japanese noodles that I loved. Shoko and I tried to solve this "sickness" together by occasionally cooking in the room. Other than the physical hunger for Japanese food, I was still running away from the holocaust. I wanted to think as little about Hiroshima as possible. The visions of injured people that were etched in my mind became detached from my feelings as if I were seeing them on a television screen. It was a strange sensation. Had there been a choice to consciously deny that I had ever lived through the ordeal, I would have asked for it. Besides, the home that I had longed to return to was gone. I could not go home ever again, no matter how homesick I might get. Hiroshima meant pain and hardship. A cycle of numbing and desensitizing became submerged with plenty of distractions in my new environment.

The Bennett faculty was headed by David Jones, the college president. I thought he resembled that powerful visionary Zionist, Ben Gurion. He was showing some visitors around one morning as I was crossing the campus green. I was swimming in an oversized hand-me-down corduroy dress as I pushed up my sleeve and extended my arm to shake his hand. A few days later, I was contacted by Mrs. Jones who sent me a few boxes full of beautiful, smaller-sized used clothes.

The political science professor, Dr. Korfield, was a Jewish survivor of Nazi persecution. She was intense in her demands for scholarly inquiry, but she was fair and compassionate at the same time. The PE and dance instructor was Armentine Douglas who had trained under Martha Graham and Ted Shawn before coming to

Bennett. Dancing to the beat of her drum was something akin to the drill calls from the Seibi Academy. No one was excused until she got it right.

The person who symbolized the elegance of the Bennett institution most was its dean, Dr. Wilma B. Player, a young woman of superior intellect and grace. I will never forget the time when I went to ask Dr. Player how I might respond to a request from the Atlanta NAACP to speak at their annual meeting. I had received the invitation shortly after the appearance of a syndicated article about my arrival at Bennett. At that time, I had had limited exposure to the delicate and dangerous climate that existed in those matters. Dr. Player averted my risk-taking without discouraging or encouraging me. Speaking with her usual calm dmeanor, she remarked that it might be an interesting experience. She was not confident, however, that it was in my interest as a student to become involved. The action might be manipulated politically, she thought. She was open to let me go, but suggested I think it over.

Without her enthusiastic support, I decided not to go. There was finesse in her not implicating anyone in particular or not detailing past victimization. I was helped to gain a perspective without being intimidated by social paranoia. This was typical of Bennett guidance. There were close personalized bonds between the faculty and the students, making each individual student feel valued.

The students were also guided by rules that governed their appearance and conduct. Other than attending classes or meals, coming and going were by permission only. Grooming was expected to be carried out with the greatest of care. For example, no one was to appear in class with frizzy hair. Once outside campus, the Bennett women distinguished themselves by elegance, always wearing a hat, a handbag, gloves, and stockings. These protocols sound antiquated today, and even then some grumbling was heard among the students. But I believe these rules were intended to protect the dignity of these women in the midst of the prejudices of their time.

The isolated setting was an insulated haven inside, but once outside, the segregation encroached immediately. I remember my first trip to the movie house with my dorm-mates. I had no idea how high they had to climb before they could be seated. It was in the attic. I must have been a nuisance as I kept walking off, thinking we were at the section where we could be seated. The girls just took it in stride, pulling me back in line, walking up the stairs. The excitement of the movie plot was sometimes interrupted by darting objects moving behind us. The resident rodents were getting ready for the leftover munchies. I found it a bit unsettling; however, no one seemed to let it spoil their evening.

Similar situations and feelings seemed to hold true in the excitement of travel, especially for going home during school holidays. "Jim Crow" cars did not hold back the students' laughter and anticipation of happy reunions. One holiday I went with Christine to her home in Orange, South Carolina. Her mother was a school teacher in an elementary school and her father owned a barber shop. They were both very laid-back people, but obviously very fond and proud of their only daughter. There was nothing dramatic about their lifestyle, yet in them I sensed a flow of steady energy. It was the same sort of strength one senses from watching farmers toil. The grains will be harvested at the end of their toil. Years later, I was not surprised to learn that Christine had become an educator serving on the faculty of a Southern university.

During summer breaks I worked as a camp counselor for children from Harlem in a program sponsored by Dr. Robinson's community center. Under the leadership of Jim Robinson, the camp had been built on the shore of a small scenic lake in Southern New Hampshire by student volunteers from the Ivy League colleges.

At camp I would braid the very short and curly hair of the children sometimes working on six or seven of them at sunrise before flag raising and breakfast. I grew accustomed to walking children back and forth to the bathroom a few times a night in my sleep. I even learned about religious prejudices from the children. One night I discovered a little Jewish girl named Joanna with long brown hair crying in my cabin for the six- and seven-year-olds. Lettricia, a quick tempered tot had just accused Joanna, saying that "her people 'killed Jesus.'" I didn't catch the point at all, startled by the amazingly early interest in exegesis.

"What's that got to do with you and Joanna, Lettricia?" I intervened.

"But it's not true, it's not true anyway," Joanna cried out in protest.

Even after I reiterated, "We mustn't go around saying things that hurt other people's feelings," I had the distinct feeling I was missing the whole point somewhere. The intensity of the charge and the protest obviously had more to do with something rooted in the culture. I wish I had understood it better then as now I can still picture the sobbing angry faces of the two girls.

Journey to the Midwest

Between semesters I found a home with a Pennsylvania family, Bill and Anna Larson and their little son, Eric. Anna had befriended the young Rev. Robinson through the church and my name had been given to them by Rev. Robinson. They lived in a modest home just outside of the town of Greensburg about thirty miles south of Pittsburgh. Bill was a machine shop foreman for Westinghouse and Ann was a housewife.

This seemingly very ordinary and unassuming couple was extraordinary in their willingness to share their home. They had hosted visitors from other lands such as China, India, and Africa. They became very involved in the life of every student, much like parents away from home. Bill would tease me about my "L" and "R" confusion, as I offered to "fly" the rice. Anna literally became my foster mother in every way, even though the only trait that we shared in common was our hobby of painting.

While studying at Bennett College and Wooster, I received many care packages from her kitchen. On holidays and birthdays she never let me forget I had a family. A little room in a house in Pennsylvania was waiting for me to come home to during school breaks. Bill and Anna were my proud family when I received my diploma from Wooster. At every point of my American journey, they were there to celebrate, observe, and encourage me. Years later, when I had children, Anna kept up with remembering the special days as well. Her care for me and my children was an uncommon gift of kindness and love.

Their steady and humble lifestyle was an anchor like the sun rising in the East and setting in the West. I had not known such stability in my life. Things had always changed or disappeared. The Larsons remained.

Time moved quickly, and by the end of my second year, a transfer to a Midwestern college, Wooster, was suggested to balance my American experience. The "other side" was not to be missed. An excellent Midwestern coed Presbyterian college was selected by Dr. Robinson. He had received an honorary degree from the institution earlier. A warm friendship existed between Jim Robinson and the college president, Dr. Howard Lowry. Dr. Lowry used to address me and ask:

"Hi Friend, how are you doing?"

"Fine sir."

"Have you heard from Jim Robinson?" he would ask, and we would chat. The subject didn't matter. Dr Lowry knew how to tap into a young mind. He was ageless. Quietly he championed the causes of reconciliation and justice. He recalled the strong objections he had encountered when he tried to recognize Jim Robinson or other minority candidates for honors from the college. One such candidate was Ms. Sawada, the founder of Elizabeth Saunder's Home, of Kamakura, Japan, who had pioneered Eurasian adoptions in occupied Japan.

Dr. Lowry appeared to be a superb symbol of his college. He gave the impression of being truly genteel. His zest for learning and sensitivity made him quite popular with the student body. He evoked a sense of trust in his students that was very similar to the trust one would find with a long time friend or family member.

Civility was everywhere. Both the faculty and the students with whom I had come in contact gave little trace of the animosity that might have existed during wartime towards a Japanese national. Doors were never slammed in my face. Questions were answered and explained. Had students felt imposed upon, they did not show it. Strangely, however, it was a very solitary place for persons who did not share the same culture or background. Most people did not reach out to understand another's differences.

In contrast to the protected haven of Bennett, where I was comfortably separated by gender and race, here was a young middle-class America, mostly white with a very few brown faces (two of whom were on the football team) or yellow. A group of us who transferred was housed in a two-story bungalow behind the football stadium. The campus was a few blocks from a small town center. I no longer had to be dressed with a hat, gloves, nylons, and handbag to visit the town. Everyday protection and respect were accorded to all students. I did not have to climb three flights of stairs to enjoy a Saturday night movie. Fried chicken dinner at the rustic and elegant Smith Inn was available to anyone who could pay for it. No one made derogatory remarks about any group. People were simply too busy keeping up with their own work. Academic commitment came before social engagements.

The theme of conformity was also evident, much as was the case in the Japanese society I had just left behind. To be well-adjusted was to become and behave like everyone else. The girls wore full-bodied crinoline under their skirts, with neatly curled hair and bobby socks. I only met the grooming requirements with the help of the hand-me-downs and donations from Anna Larson's friends and family.

While the racial and cultural differences were non-issues here, I wished for interest in some cultural differences. I remember there was one such attempt made by a housemate one December evening. Sally, who transferred from San Francisco, asked in the middle of carol singing over hot apple cider and popcorn, if I would lead "Silent Night" in Japanese first. As I began to sing it, I realized it was for my benefit that she had made the suggestion.

There were a few other women with whom I was able to form a genial friendship. Mary was a warm and giving young woman from Brooklyn who resented the encroaching world of conformity which she apparently experienced growing up as an only daughter of a

Protestant minister in a large urban parish. I used to tell her that she should see a society even *more* tightly watched over, such as the one I had just left. To relieve her tension, Mary would suddenly belt out a reverberating note or an aria in the middle of our walks on the campus. I remember her wearing an old brown fur coat past its prime, ready to fall apart. She stood like a diva in a soft Ohio rain looking so very happy. I had no idea then that Mary's life was to end in a little over ten years when she would die from an unsuspected embolism in her brain.

It was also at Wooster that I began to notice a sense of disconnection, no matter how hard I tried to overcome it. It was like having an electrical cord, but being unable to find an outlet to plug it into. In one of my psychology classes a professor ran a survey of students' social attitude towards ethnicity. The students were asked to rate their willingness to associate, work, or play with, and date or marry members of different groups. I felt that everything being equal, that is, if the individual was a decent person, I could reply in the affirmative to all of the questions.

In discussing the results, the professor disclosed he had to throw out one survey which gave indiscriminately positive answers to all groups which surely was an error. He then proceeded to show, with an extremely small exception, that almost no one had crossed the racial boundary and that most preferred associations with one's own kind. It was a predictable conclusion, but I was dismayed not to have been counted in the survey because my response had been classified as invalid.

Another event that had a similar effect took place when an esteemed Wooster alum, a Manhattan Project physicist, spoke in the chapel. A tall gentleman with distinguished features, Dr. Compton mesmerized the chapel audience as he spoke about his past activities and about his brother, also a physicist on the Project. He appeared brilliant and decisive. I did not know if he knew that a woman who sat terrified by his presence was in the audience. I was unable to detect any regrets over the deliberate choice of civilian targets.

It was one thing to be in a country which brought my home

nation to its knees. But it was quite another to be in the presence of one of the masterminds behind the creation of the weapon capable of the unparalleled destruction of humans. I asked silently, "Dr. Compton, do you know how we died, and that we are still dying now from your creation, sir?"

My terror, however, was not fueled by the past and the present reality of warfare. I could not change any part of those aspects anyway. It was the distance that separated me from Dr. Compton that left me horrified. Had he indicated any sensitivity to or consideration for victims of his proud project, I would have felt less terror.

Years later, when I recalled that morning of the physicist's return to Wooster, I wished that I had spoken to the esteemed scientist, confronting him with the questions that I was never able to ask. When my chapel attendance-taker asked me about my reaction afterward, I smiled in the same way that I always did. I think my lips quivered a little though; I was still shaken but I kept silent.

By this time I had been in the country for two years, but my mastery of the English language was far from sufficient, lagging behind my own expectations. Working with the new faculty and gaining their confidence was an uphill task given my language limitations. My elementary speed of study was insufficient to meet the challenge of independent study, research, and writing. In my junior year, I ventured to write on the concept of "self," and in my senior year, I tried to write on the human relations factor in productivity. Both subjects were objects of my intense curiosity, but much beyond my linguistic ability in data search or analysis. I really needed much more than independent research.

Fortunately, there were not restrictions like lights out at night and study hours at Bennett, but my speed was still at a crawling pace in reading and writing. I did not know then that these were problems many Asian students faced because of their having to overcome vast linguistic differences. I held *myself* responsible and deficient. I suspect that at least some of my faculty did as well.

The frustrations and embarrassment I experienced culminated

in a conference one afternoon. I sat in my advisor's office with a suddenly developed runny nose. I had not taken a handkerchief or tissue with me, but on his desk was a box of tissues. I sniffled trying to keep from dripping. I was too shy to ask if I might have a tissue. My advisor looked on undisturbed. Finally, the liquid from my nostrils gave in to gravity. I grabbed the only thing I had, a pair of woolen gloves. I wiped under my nose with them. Nearly forty years have passed since that afternoon, but the scene comes back to me as one of ineptitude and shame on my part and a puzzle over my "independence" to the finish. I can still see the faint amusement on the professor's face.

Outside of school, foreign students were frequently asked to speak to local church groups. During these engagements people often asked questions about my experience with the atomic bomb. People were interested in my description of the event. It did not take long before I found myself feeling numb and mechanical going through a robotic speech whenever the question came up. It was as if I were describing it as a bystander or a third person. I still felt quite anxious each time, and grew weary of discussing the subject. Whenever I was asked where I was from, I started replying that I was born in Tokyo, and I came from Japan.

Even around friends, authentic discussion about the war experiences was difficult. How does one describe terror and grief to those who never lived through such horrific losses? It was burdensome to think about them, much less discuss them. At times, humming melodies of Mama's favorite songs was about the only way that I could bring back any feelings. Vascillating in the maze of resurfacing fears, the direction of my study abroad was becoming obscure.

After a summer of working in the Inner City Protestant Parish, I headed for McCormick Theological Seminary, a quiet little haven on the north side of Chicago in 1956. Before my arrival in Chicago, the city's reputation as the home of Al Capone and company had reached me and even my relatives back in Japan, who had watched Elliot Ness speaking in Japanese on a black and white television. I had tasted a prelude to Chicago by living on Woodland Avenue in Cleveland, the poorest street in the country. There was pounding on our door sometimes in the middle of the night, calling for names of women from whom the callers had received pleasure. Apparently, the women had moved on and the men had not realized that the mission had taken over the place. We sometimes had to step over men stooped on the stairway by the outside entrance, perhaps homeless, and most likely very lost in the task of simply surviving.

I began to see an America that neither Bennett nor Wooster had shown me. While stepping over these men, I remembered the people who lay dying in Hiroshima and in the surrounding towns to which they had been carried. I remembered the orphaned children and the men without work and shelter who were also found sleeping outdoors. When I traveled with my father I saw their faces and broken spirits. I did not know how the homeless Americans got to where they were, but I did know that the homeless Japanese had been driven to where they were by the bomb. Broken dreams and lost lives were in those bodies we were stepping over on Woodland Avenue.

12

Shadow of Hiroshima

Chalmer's Place

The small residence space for the female seminarians called Ewing Hall was actually the two upper floors above the classrooms and offices, which were also connected to the chapel. The only time I had to step outside was to walk out to the dining hall where I'd pass a quaint little inner garden sanctuary called Chalmer's Place. Faculty houses lined this garden, starting with a larger and separate house for the seminary president.

From my window I looked directly out to tranquil Chalmer's Place. It was particularly serene in or after the rain. Leaves sparkled with rain drops much like the trees in my old garden in Hiroshima. I had come to the seminary after a long unrewarding quest for answers that might help me to have steady energy and to experience a joy in living. I thought to myself that if a life had been spared when so many were not, it must have been for a reason more worthwhile than mine, which consisted of barely making it from one day to the next.

My roommate, Mary, from Omaha, Nebraska, was gracious and beautiful like a well-raised traditional Japanese woman. Her movements were soft and light. Her belongings were neatly kept in the small space we shared. She made all of her clothes. They were stylish and versatile with little change of accessories. I continued to learn the nuances of culture when the subject of racial differences came up. She said that in Omaha more than a few shared the sentiment of a man who said, "I hate prejudice, and I hate niggers." "Hatred" sounded like a very strong word. It was a chilling thought.

I wondered about how they felt toward the Japanese then. She told me that she had gone to school with Japanese American girls. They associated with one another without any barriers in school. But she would not have greeted them on the streets, and the Japanese girls would not have expected her to acknowledge them. The explanation was not very clear to me until a faint memory from my childhood in Hiroshima came back.

Long before our city was destroyed, I remembered how confused a neighbor girl, Kikue, became when I was not allowed to invite her into the house. I met her one day outside the wall. We played games of ball and beanbags called *ojami*. We promised each other future fun and games soon. She came to see me a few days later. When I started to show her where she could leave her *getta* sandals, I was called away. I was expected elsewhere. It turned out that Kikue was not allowed in the house. I asked Mama why I couldn't play with my playmates inside just as I did outside, like we used to in our little house in Tokyo. She said that the family preferred that children's play be kept outside. Kikue kept returning a few more times. She said, "I know our family is different from your family, that's the reason I can't come in, isn't it?"

I told her the same thing Mama had said the first time. On her second return, there was a garden full of cousins playing cops and robbers swinging from the trees, jumping from the rocks. She wanted to be a part of it, and watched us play for a long time. No one paid much attention. After that she stopped coming over.

At the end of the first semester, my roommate became engaged to a young farm manager back home. She decided to leave the seminary. I was invited to her wedding, but the trip was more than I could afford at the time. I sent her a Japanese lacquer box for a wedding gift. She sent me back a tape of their ceremony, and expressed the wish that I had been there. I pictured her in an elegant white gown of her own creation. Her children would be well cared for with God-fearing decent parents. I wondered if they would be playing with the children of other "colors."

The letters from home became fewer and fewer as Papa and my uncle continued in their struggle to bring back the Tamura name to the level it had been at in my grandfather's time. It was not to be achieved. The market for sewing needles was diminishing despite Papa's and my uncle's passion for and loyalty to the company that my grandfather had founded. The factory and the machinery were burned down twice; once by the bombing and the second time by a fire suspected of having been set by a disgruntled former employee. The debts were accumulating. Finally, a decision was reached to diversify and to export their technology to underdeveloped countries. Papa began to specialize in building and teaching needle manufacturing technology in other Asian countries.

His letters were written in neat handwriting. He told me how much he regretted his inability to help me. He had lost his share of his father's estate under the old constitution that stated that the eldest male heir was to receive all of the inheritance in order to look after the rest of the family. After MacArthur's occupation and the change in the Japanese constitution, his elder brother was exonerated from this responsibility, Papa being shortchanged by the new law as well.

Papa would write about how he wanted to pass on to me a part of the proceeds, should he succeed in getting a small share back from his brother. He could not fathom how a young girl without assistance from her family could possibly make it on her own in a foreign land even with a scholarship. Years later, after both Papa and my uncle had passed away, Papa's share was gifted back by Cousin Kumiko. Ironically, even when Papa's dream finally came true, a share in the gift never reached me.

While Papa toiled away in faraway countries like India and Indonesia, teaching technologies his father had brought into Hiroshima long ago, I was hitting books about ancient oracles and the spiritual world. Aside from the routine survey courses there was a wide latitude of specialization in which one could pursue pathways other than the ministry. I, of course, was there for my own salvation. The combination of theological education and social work appealed to me most. I struggled through heaps of materials defining the power and the presence of God, having the childlike fancy that I was going to be touched by a magic wand of blessing and enlightenment by which my fragmented sense of life would come together. Nevertheless, the lack of energy I had begun to notice at Wooster gradually increased.

The only thing that came together was a realization that the search was endless. The concepts of the "Creation" and the "Fall of Man" followed by "salvation through Christ" ran circles around me without touching my soul. I was stuck in the Fall. I had experienced love, human love, that was taken away. What did my mother and Cousin Hideyuki ever do to have "Fallen" where they did? The heat that burned into Hideyuki's flesh and the concrete that fell on Mama and the maggots that moved in the living charred bodies before my eyes could not be restored even in the light of the Divine. Remembering the scene even for a fraction of a second took away my own dignity and terrified me to my very core. The blinding light that flashed through us and turned our homes and families to ashes and us into the living dead was made by men but was surely within God's realm of knowledge and power.

I could not be objective in deciphering the message from any text. Whether or not the Fall of Man or the demand for salvation and reconciliation came into the picture made little difference to me at that time. I could not have related or responded to the concept no matter how hard I tried to personalize it. Whether God's love surpassed beyond all human love or not, I wanted far less. The love I wanted was human love—even just a little bit. I craved peace of mind, and a rest from endless running.

Not even abstractly could I envisage burning and crushed people or the ailing *hibakusha* (atomic bomb survivors) as being messengers or symbols of anything other than death itself. The worst part was the "living dead" part of myself within me—a perpetual internal dying because I could not forget what I had seen.

A prayer of praise and gratitude had to be a hallow one. How could one sing a "Joyful, joyful . . ." with an energy level as low as the heights on one's knees, trembling with a fear that would not cease. The fear had started to creep up sometime during my Wooster days. News of the residual harm from radiation was slowly getting out after the Allied Occupation of Japan ended with the San Francisco Treaty. The silence was lifting and the lasting harm that the people had suffered since the exposure to radiation was becoming unveiled. I tried to minimize any alarm by consciously denying that I suffered any ill effects. I tried to convince myself that if I did not give any credence to the reports I would be safe. The label *hibakusha,* therefore, did not apply to me. My denial was so strong that it is curious to me that I remained fearful at all.

The free-floating sense of fear did not abate, but increased without warning. The sound of firearms, any kind of fire, or a sudden loud noise could send my heart racing. Gradually, the fears became wardens of my own personal prison without entrance or exit. Pretending that I had not suffered a casualty was obviously not the answer.

Sometimes I wondered if most people had thought of the civilian casualties in Hiroshima as "the heathens be damned" in this connection. My grandfather, a "heathen," showed extreme kindness to a foreign cleric in distress when it was uncommon to do so. To him a servant of God was to be respected regardless of his religion. My grandfather used to teach us by reading from the holy text about the ills of selfish demands and interest and the Grace that would be granted us when we abandoned our selfish deeds and thoughts. How should such gentle thoughts be damned as heathen?

Around me were serious men and women dedicated to preparing themselves for the ministry. Had I screamed a loud "help," they would have come to my aid. I don't think I could have put into words exactly what it was that I was looking for. Perhaps a touch of human frailty or authentic interest in another human being was all that I wished for. In the midst of the faithful there was an agonizing soul among them, wanting more than anything a warmth of an authentic friendship that would not disappear.

My silent scream must have been heard. I can recall a handful of young women who each shared a part of herself with me in ways that I still enjoy today. Maggie, a widow from Dubuque, Iowa, was so open with her ups and downs that she helped others forget their downs. Joann from Boise, Idaho, was an earthy country girl with the sharpest wit and an amazing storytelling talent. People were magnetized by her charm. Arlene, a daughter of a missionary to Japan, was particularly caring, and a very willing listener. Her courage in speaking up for her convictions was impressive. Winifred from Oberlin was twice my size but shy and reserved. She was steadfast and trustworthy. Barbara from the near west side of Chicago was the giver of wisdom. I could always go to Barbara when I needed a balanced opinion. Like no other, Arlene from northern Indiana accorded me great respect for my intellectual prowess. We would exchange our ideas into the wee hours of the night after our work and studies.

I could count on any of these women to be there for me during my stay at the seminary. Their caring provided me with an immeasurable gift of spiritual sustenance.

By that time other young seminarians had found their way to my dorm. I became particularly friendly with a young man from Wisconsin whose father had died of Parkinson's disease while he was still in his teens. His revealing the grief in his young life sparked a commonality between us, though I had not said very much about my own experiences. Our friendship, however, seemed to cause conflict within himself as well. One evening he blurted out in the lounge that he could not commit himself to a Canaanite woman.

I was quite taken aback both at being addressed as an outsider and the idea that a commitment was being entertained without my participation. In the presence of other men and women in the small lounge there was little privacy, perhaps by choice. I had not been taught how to respond in situations like this except to feel very embarrassed and remain silent. But I found myself actually speaking to his point. It may have been at that moment that I started my therapist's career as I recall mirroring his statement and guessing that he might be feeling guilty about his own conflicting feelings. Later, I was pleasantly surprised by a lovely invitation from his mother to come and visit their home. Although the friendship faded, I remember the episode as one of my early journeys in understanding others' grief and the affect on my life.

From time to time visitors from Japan also came past the iron gate of the seminary, prompted by Papa who himself could not break away from his duties. My visitors were all equally relieved to find me in everyday attire rather than in a nun's habit. To them, entrance into a theological seminary represented an extraordinary separation from secular society. Mr. Matsuda of Mazda fame from Hiroshima was a younger alum of Keio University. He and Papa belonged to its alumni club, Mita-Kai, in Hiroshima. His innovative visions in automobile-making were quite apparent as he discussed his interest in German engines with passion over bowls of noodles and plates of sushi.

Papa's cousin, Cousin Nishikawa, was also a frequent visitor after his company entered in a licensing agreement with a Chicago company, bringing his staff training to Chicago. Cousin Nishikawa loved steaks at the Stockyard Inn. He, too, was extraordinarily ahead of his time. He and his older brother turned the rubber goods manufacturing company founded by my grandfather into a multinational company producing weather stripping for automobiles.

My visitors from Japan would bring messages from Papa and news of the relatives. These few hours we would spend together succeeded in bringing me back to Hiroshima. Once Cousin Nishikawa, who is an energetic and upbeat business executive, recalled his war experience of the day the bomb was dropped. He had been mobilized to work in a factory as a student just outside the city. He struggled towards home that day chased by fire, lending his hand to burned and mangled people who were mostly beyond help. Home had never been so far a journey. Finally, exhausted, he collapsed on a grass patch by the Ota river and spent the night there, his hair singed and his entire body covered with soot. By that point in his story, Cousin Nishikawa's usually masculine and confident face had turned somber and lusterless as he gazed in space and said it was "very very hard." We never touched the subject again.

By the second year of seminary my graduate program became a collaborative effort with the area professional schools of social work. My studies in human services were something concrete that I could relate to and actually enjoy. After a year of working with teen groups at the Erie Neighborhood House, I signed up for a joint graduate program with the University of Chicago. As the course requirements increased in the university curriculum, I began to spend more and more time on the South Side. To save time I decided to relocate near the campus. The International House on the university campus seemed just the place. Leaving behind the quaint and peaceful Chalmer's Place, I headed for my new environment on the South Side.

The International World

My plain and small room held just enough space for a single bed, a desk with a chair, a lamp, and a lounge chair. It was conducive to quiet study but not to the congregation of friends as in a college dorm. It was more like a modest room in a convent. For the first time, however, there was diversity of cultures and races around me. No longer did anyone stand out because of non-Caucasian features or heavily accented English. Ideas and activities were the focus. One's ethnicity was a respected identity. People still looked at their own ethnic group as a family, though, and the Japanese were no exception. Doctors, researchers, students, young and old, men and women bonded together. It was an unlikely mix of people who probably would not have come together had they met back home.

With a moment's notice we would jump into an old Hillman sedan owned by a newly arrived physicist and go to movies, visit museums or the zoo, or go for noodle soup at a Chinese restaurant on 63rd Street. One person's trouble was everyone else's. We mourned deeply when the wife of a visiting scientist from Kyoto died during heart surgery. They had been married because of romantic love rather than the customary arranged marriage.

"If I hadn't wished for a cure," he lamented, "she would be alive today, she didn't want to do it, it's all my fault." He blamed himself for having placed his hope in the advanced American medicine over her doctors in Japan. He was a broken man who could not be comforted. We tried.

He was not consoled by any of us telling him that we understood how it felt to be in his shoes. I could not bring myself to tell him that I had once held myself responsible for Mama's death because I had insisted on coming home the day before our city was struck down. I did not know that the *Enola Gay* would be on its way with its grave mission. I would have been ecstatic to have remained in the country with all its lice infestation and starvation, had I only known. So would have my best friend, Miyoshi. She would have been alive herself. Our scientist friend had a noble cause, his wife's welfare. Mine was one I considered selfish and childish—I just wanted to be at home with Mama.

I tried to tell him how legitimate his high hopes were, and that there was no way he could have known it wouldn't work. It was to no avail. He still blamed himself. He was lost without his best friend. He remained solitary for the remainder of his stay in the International House that year, after which he returned to Japan. How well I knew that feeling. It was comforting to know that his situation was unlike mine in Hiroshima. His family, his town, and his work were still in existence and there was no fear of toxic contamination. The complete disappearance of everything was still too difficult for me to think about.

Welcome as it was to be back with my compatriots, there was an unexpected downside. Even before the untimely death of the scientist's spouse, I noticed a strange phenomenon occurring. An image of Mama kept reappearing in my mind out of nowhere. Her hair was in disarray and her eyes showed little emotion. She was wearing her *nemaki* (sleep wear) kimono but I could not tell if she was ill or just weary. An old folk belief held that visions of deceased loved ones were indications of their souls' wandering, or that they were trying to send messages to the living. I had no idea what Mama's messages might have been. It was scary to find myself alone in the quiet hours of the dark night with Mama returning stripped of joy or energy. The experience was so strange that I could not share it even with my close Japanese colleagues.

When these images recurred, I tried to remember the happy faces of Mama, but it was of no use. I was no longer a small child. I needed a bonding image for the young adult I was becoming. As soon as I would succeed in recapturing her young happy days with Papa, something within me would whisper, "remember how it ended." In the end, the wandering of my own soul was cast upon the very image of my mother.

Another vision that recurred unabated was the very vivid physical sensation that I was dying. It happened for the first time during the summer we returned to Hiroshima three years after the atom bomb explosion. I was lying on a *tatami* mat on the night of *Obon* (an August ceremony honoring the dead among the Buddhists) just having returned from the lantern lighting ceremony at the Tokuoji Temple. Suddenly, I was gripped with the most awful sensation of the moment of death. My body was actually simulating what it might feel like to die. I could not stand it. I wanted to scream.

I asked Aunt Fumiko rather insipidly if she had ever experienced anything like that. She said she hadn't. There was no way to suppress it, and my knowledgeable aunt hadn't even experienced it. Aunt Fumiko had taught me the "how to" of managing many challenges from the monthly feminine visitor to cooking perfect rice. This was one without precedent but repeated itself time and again. Like the vision of Mama in sleepwear, it came without warning. It chose no particular time of the day or no particular location—practicum hours, study time, or anywhere. I would stiffen up in alarm and groan in desperation. It was as if the voice of the living dead within me was finally speaking out. For my consciousness, however, the sensation was sheer terror.

By this time I was also progressing in my graduate work, and enlarging my understanding of common human needs, casework theories, psychosocial pathologies, and child placement with the inevitable impact of separation anxieties. The voices and the faces of my teachers, Ms. Towle, Pearlman, Schultz, Drs. Skolanski and Litner still return because they opened the doors to deeper understanding of the human experiences. Perhaps because I was raised by parents who were influenced by Western thoughts, these explanations provided an intellectual understanding of my early life and my clients' behavior. Still all the insights were not sufficient to lighten my psychological burdens.

Whether in the chapel or in the classroom neither my prayers nor my newly acquired knowledge brought lasting respite. I blamed no one but myself for this condition, holding myself deficient. I now wonder if blaming myself had a dimension of preserving my dignity, however infinitesimal.

I began to focus my efforts more and more on the differences that I might be able to make in the lives of my clients. Perhaps I was clinging to a dimension of the human condition that I felt I could still do something about. To help a fellow human being, however, was not so simple, either.

An old retired lawyer of Polish descent who lived in a tiny room by the 63rd Street El track longed to have a pair of sturdy galoshes. He loved to take walks in the snow. There was no allowance in his Aid budget. I wanted to buy them for him myself. My request was gently denied by a sympathetic supervisor on the basis that the rules had to be kept the same for all recipients.

In another instance, I sat in the kitchen of a young ADC mother with a seven-year-old boy. There was a male caller with a boxer's physique. Missing his name I started to ask him, after my own introduction, what he said his name was. He replied promptly, "I didn't say." That was the end of our conversation. A few years later, I saw the same mother in a grocery store. She appeared more settled and secure with her son. Much to my amazement she greeted me enthusiastically saying how helpful I had been years before.

In spite of my ignorance or naiveté about the fabric of American life, I managed to get through my training in placing and supervising foster homes, counseling children and their parents. One of the work requirements was the ability to drive a car in order to make home visits and other work related trips. I had to have someone teach me how to drive. A buddy from the Philippines suggested the name of a young man whose character had been highly recommended.

That's how I met Robert D. Snider from Weiser, Idaho, in the lounge of the International House. When my friend Nene pointed him out to me, I remembered this young man with very blue eyes and slightly receding front blond hair frequently engaged in serious discussions with the men residents. I hesitated to just walk up to him, so I asked Nene if she might ask for me. After receiving a favorable signal I told Robert I needed help and that his character reference had preceded him. Robert was actually quite shy. His face turned red at being singled out, but he quickly added that he would be happy to teach me how to drive. I also learned that he was a master's degree candidate in political science on a Woodrow Wilson Scholarship.

I had been told that teaching a person how to drive was a very trying experience. One could not have known this from Robert. His patience, as Japanese would say, "was like the Buddha's." My feel for easing the clutch and pushing the gas pedal was so awkward that it caused the vehicle to move like it had the hiccups. He took it in good humor saying that everyone starts out awkwardly. He was never irritated.

We began to recognize each other outside of the practices and a friendship evolved without strain. One thing that stood out in this friendship was the ease with which he respected my boundaries. I remembered some casual acquaintances who were quick to hold my hand and intrude into my physical space. I would then have to explain the different practices in our cultures, as if to apologize but feeling altogether uncomfortable. An aberration was not expected.

One afternoon Robert felt that I was ready for the driving test. In order to be sure to cover all the maneuvers, he drove me to the test site on the far South Side where the miniature slopes and parking spaces were laid out. I was concentrating very hard on one of my weaker points of which there were many, but particularly on my parallel parking. On the third or fourth try, I thought that I had completed a perfect backing between the two rubber poles. From the rearview mirror I saw the flag wagging slightly. Just at that instant the sound of a small obscenity jumped out of my mouth. I realized immediately that I had just spoken in a way I had never done before in any polite company. I looked at Robert in great embarrassment, wishing I hadn't uttered the sound. He chuckled at first, raising his eyebrows. Then something I hadn't expected in my wildest dreams happened. He bent over and kissed me. I had forgotten that I was supposed to recite for him my customary speech about Japanese practices. A mild breeze passed over our warm cheeks as we looked at each other more surprised now with the reaction than I was with the word I had uttered just seconds before.

What was kindled in a driving range that afternoon turned into a growing trust and a strong bond between a young American man from an Idaho farm and a Japanese woman from Hiroshima. The distance between our two worlds was vast and yet we were very much alike under our very different appearances and dispositions. Robert was quiet and deliberate. I was actually more outspoken than he. I tended to move quickly and more decisively. But we shared many inward traits. We were drawn to the same type of music, schools of thought, people, food, and the kind of dignity we accorded each other. In short we were a pair of different peas in the same pod, as comfortable together as a tree and its branches. Our differences complemented each other effortlessly.

The grotesque images and the persistent lethargy I had often suffered began to fade. Laughter seemed to take their place. I even tried to recreate gravy and fried chicken after hearing about his mother's legendary culinary feats that used to melt in his mouth. I had no idea how they were made. Neither did Robert. We experimented following a recipe from a cookbook.

Once we were caught by a storm while driving near a forest preserve. The forceful thunder and lightning were frightening but Robert's comfortable presence took the edge off my dread. The light was beckoning from beyond the horizon finally as I tried to forget and break away from my inner struggles.

Shameful and embarrassing memories of my past were the last thing I thought of when I was with Robert. He had no idea that there was a drenching history behind me other than a simple comment about my having survived the Hiroshima bombing in which my mother had been killed. I wish today that I had shared more so that he would have had a better idea and understanding of all that I had gone through. His support would have been there.

By the time my professional training came to a close Robert and I had come to agree on a permanent commitment. We became engaged when his master's thesis in political science neared completion. I had not given up on the idea of contributing to the welfare of my own society back home. I felt a strong obligation to share what I had learned in human services. I also felt strongly that our bond should receive blessings from both of our families even if it took time. Robert was more independent minded on the subject. He was entirely comfortable making his own decisions for himself alone.

As a child and throughout my teens I used to tell my friends and family that I would never marry. No one took me seriously, including me. I was seriously doubtful about the permanence of anything on this planet. It took this young man to bring me closest to a changing of attitude. In the midst of an agonizing personal journey I dedicated my future to be spent in his presence wherever it might take us. While Robert was preparing to continue his doctoral course at a West coast university, I headed home to rework my unfinished agenda of re-entry into my own family and society, and to win support for my marriage to a foreign young man. In our commitment to work out many options we had not set a time table for the latter as yet.

On the way to the port of departure I made a brief stop in Weiser, Idaho, for a visit with Robert's family. I saw the origin of my friend's dignity and steadfastness in the loving relationship between his parents. The alfalfa fields stretched wide, filling the basin of the mountain ranges. The beauty and the harshness of mighty nature combined with the dignity of one man's work to dwell in them were reflected in Robert's father. This tall handsome man with graying hair, a warm shine in his eyes, and a great presence about him was not without some misgiving about his son's choice. Robert's quiet and gentle mother stayed in the background busying herself with the food preparation and routine household tasks. We only exchanged a few incidental words during my short stay, but I had the sense that she wanted me to have a comfortable visit.

Like my grandfather's daily teaching from the holy texts, Robert's father read from his text, the Bible. His candid prayer reflected an understandable apprehension about our situation. His siblings, an older sister and a younger brother, could not have been more supportive. I could sense their warmth in reaching out to me. A seed of uncertainty was nevertheless planted as my journey home continued.

13

The Darkening Shadow

Tadaima kaerimashita
(I have returned now)

The entourage of the welcoming party stood behind Papa who was calling out my name, "Hideko, here, here." Little Cousin Kumiko had grown so tall that I saw her smiling face first, a few inches above the others. She was standing next to my stepmother, Tetsuko, and an old classmate, Miyoko, from the Hiroshima Mission School. Miyoko happened to be in Tokyo living with her sister and joined my family at Papa's invitation. We had been friends since the Kabe days right after the bombing. Her father had been a well respected plant manager for the Tamura Industrial Group before the war. Though the war effort nearly closed our factories, and Miyoko's father went on to become a successful business man on his own, there has always been a very warm tie between the two families.

"*Tadaima* (now this moment) *kaerimashita* (I've come home to you)."

I made my deep bow with great depth of emotion. It had been ten years since I last saw Japan from the deck of an American freighter. The prematurely aging man before me had been so much younger looking when we waved our last good-byes. Back then we must have had doubts as to whether we would ever see each other again.

As if the eternal moment of truth were with us, and proved to be too overwhelming, Papa quickly led us out to the airport skyline lounge. As we followed Papa, we broke into small chatter asking and telling each other simultaneously how good it was to find each other in the huge crowd.

"You're going to rest first with a drink of soda."

I had already had more than enough food and drink on the plane but of course I accepted Papa's treat. It was also a ceremonial occasion. We sat speaking a few words at a time as we observed each others' changed appearances. Papa's hair had thinned out and his teary eyes had grown smaller and more deeply sunken. One could detect that hard years had taken their toll.

I hardly recognized my cousin. She had grown into a woman of large frame towering over me. A shy little girl who used to look up to me was now a fully developed young woman wearing makeup. Tetsuko-san seemed ageless looking exactly as I remembered her, regal and quietly in charge. She spoke briefly with reserve. Miyoko also seemed unchanged with her beautiful fair complexion and lovely features. A touch of resolve and discipline was mirrored in her thoughtful eyes. She had cared for her father and after his death she put her younger sister through school before she undertook her own college education. This was no ordinary sacrifice. She watched me search for words of reentry back into their world.

I was wearing a new woolen suit of blue and gray tweed purchased from Marshall Fields, a reputable store in Chicago. My head was covered by a blue feathered hat with a short veil like Mama used to don. It was a far cry from the secondhand outfit I wore when I left Japan. But there obviously were more changes than mere clothes in all of us. We focused, instead, on the changes in the landscapes in Tokyo, Hiroshima, and everywhere. No doubt my changes were more apparent to them than theirs to me. We continued to seek out old connections, friends, families, and places.

Slowly, I was entering back into their lives. Hideo, my stepbrother, who stayed behind in Hiroshima, excelled in school, ranking at the top of his class in the Hiroshima University Lab School. Uncle Hisao, on the other hand, had developed a large tumor at the base of his throat around the site of his earlier injury from the bomb. Papa gestured to show where the large swelling had occurred under Uncle Hisao's chin. Papa had written very briefly about it just before I left Chicago.

"What do the doctors say, Papa?" I asked.

"They don't seem to really know, maybe it's a goiter."

"Can they cut it out maybe?" I was afraid to ask in Cousin Kumiko's presence if it was cancerous.

"Well, the doctors told him that he would be running the risk of possibly damaging some of the delicate nerves controlling the facial muscles"

"You mean he could be drooling and all that?"

"That was the gist of it, and my brother wouldn't have it." Cousin Kumiko's eyes were downcast.

"So what *is* he doing about it?" I wondered. I definitely understood my uncle's apprehension. This was the first-born son of Grandfather Hidetaro who had brought industry to Hiroshima. Uncle Hisao was a revered public servant in his own right, having served on the city council of Hiroshima in the war years and after. He would probably die before losing control over his speech or ability to relate to the public with dignity.

"The doctors suggested that about the only thing left was radiation treatment," Papa replied.

"Is that safe Papa? Wasn't that what killed everyone?" I was apprehensive. "Well, apparently in small dosages it could shrink the tumor." The subject had subdued the entire company by then. We drifted off to other topics.

Grandmother Tamano had passed away during my absence. I remembered her voice, as we said good-byes while standing on the platform of the Hiroshima station. She had said that she was afraid we would never see each other again if she let go of my hand. I remembered the grip and the warmth of her hand like she was there in front of me now. We never would see each other again just as she had feared. Grandmother Tamano had been suffering from chronic abdominal pain since the bomb exposure. Doctors were unable to find the cause. She died without knowing what had ailed her. I asked about Aunt Kiyoko. She had been looking after her mother, and still shared the house that had been built on the old estate site.

"She'd be so happy to see you," said Papa.

"Is she in good health? She used to be sickly during the war, remember?"

I pictured my once intimidating aunt who warned in a stern voice when I told her about my initial interest in Bennett College, that I was not to bring home a *kuro-chan* (a "darkie"). I remember being stunned by her suggestion, and replying to her that I had had no thoughts of bringing anyone home with me and that my sole purpose in going to America was for my education. It was fortunate that no other family member had intimated any comments of this sort then or since, as they might have tempted me to defy them just to prove my own youthful and self-righteous boundaries and show that I had a mind of my own.

Papa was anxious to take me around and feed me more. He wanted to know what I had missed most in food. My answer naturally was, "Sushi." Then sushi it was, as we sat at a sushi bar nearby to feast again. We climbed the Tokyo Tower for a spectacular view of rebuilt Tokyo, but it looked just like any other metropolis and not the Tokyo of old that had been so dear to me and Mama. The chrysanthemum at Meiji Shrine was the next stop; there it was restful and the cool breeze smelled like something from the long past. Poor Papa with his thin, small frame walked hastily from one spot to another, trying his best to make the day my warmest welcome home.

We spent the night in a hotel and rode the train home the next morning. Looking out the window, I saw that the countryside was unchanged. The golden rice fields had been harvested and the fall leaves colored the mountain landscapes. Familiar sights were coming back to me. In less time than it had taken me to drive from Chicago to San Francisco, I had left my American experiences and landed on my hometown soil, Hiroshima, yet another world.

Aunt Kiyoko, Uncle Hisao, Aunt Fumiko, and Mama's brother

Uncle I-chan, and his sister, Auntie Kozue, were all at the station waiting for our arrival. I was ashamed of having thought of my Aunt Kiyoko's sternness when I saw her bent back and her aged appearance. Uncle Hisao's lower face was quite swollen. "I'm under the care of a doctor, you know," he spoke as if to apologize for his changed appearance. His condition had not weakened him but his vibrant laughter and energetic strides were no longer there. He was a changed man with something terribly wrong.

My little stepbrother had also grown from a toddler to a young teen. He was nearly as tall as Papa. He occupied my old room, sharing it with Cousin Kumiko whom he called, "Sis." I used to carry him on my back after school and take him for walks by the river bank. Now that he had become a big boy who seldom spoke I was lost as to how to reach out to him. The sudden reappearance of his stepsister must have been equally awkward for him.

I have no recollection today of all the gifts I brought back to my family on my return trip, except for those I had picked out for my stepbrother, a Parker pen and a trendy sweater that I carefully selected after several days' search. When I gave them to him, I saw him nodding, but I could not tell if the gifts had pleased him at the time. I simply judged his lack of expression to be that of a typical young Japanese boy. Sometime later, I saw him in his new sweater as if he were quite pleased.

I bowed deeply to everyone, repeating, *"Tadaima kaerimashita,"* and received their response, *"Yoku kaetta"* (It is good you returned) each time. The most important *"Tadaima"* was to be spoken at the Tokuoji Temple in front of the family grave. The ashes collected from the rubble of the building where Mama had been last seen had been placed in an urn under the grave stone. Papa drove me there immediately.

To be back in Hiroshima was relatively quick and simple physically and even socially under Papa's guidance. But there was no word to describe the sense of pathos I felt standing before the family grave.

"Hideko-chan, give Mama your *Tadaima* greeting, she'd be so glad."

That's all he said as he lighted incense sticks and placed a small bunch of flowers in the specially designed receptacle inset in the gravestone. I had come to this grave to say, *"Itte kimasu* (I am leaving), Mama," also at Papa's urging. It was as if he were trying his best to keep her presence for me by showing her our respect. I never could speak of the frightening images I had had of Mama or the sensation of dying that I had suffered or of how unspeakably difficult it was for me to think of her dying moment. The latter was inevitably connected to coming to her grave, which I had not accepted was hers. Hers was somewhere in the physical and spiritual universe of 1945 eons ago. A part of me had stayed there. I felt myself becoming more uneasy as we drove off.

The round of *"Tadaima kaerimashita"* was repeated time and again as I went around reporting my safe return to nearly twenty Tamura relatives. Following the traditional practice, I presented to each family a gift—a beautifully carved and stained tray—as a greeting and rekindling of our renewed ties. I wore my blue tweed suit and a veiled hat each time. Sitting on my knees while wearing nylons was a strain on my hose as well as on my leg muscles after ten years of relaxing them on chairs. But I managed small chats with even ailing relatives at their bedsides, like Cousin Nishikawa's father, Uncle Bunji, the CEO of the Nishikawa Rubber Industries. Once a powerful chieftain, he was in frail health like Uncle Hisao. He was happy to see me, repeating with a smile, "Well done, Child, well done."

For those who had departed this world while I was gone, I burned incense praying for their souls' peace and for their protection over me as we believed them to be our ancestral guardians. My relatives were eager hosts and appeared surprised that I acted pretty much like anyone of my age who had never left the country. Some folks even complimented me for my change, observing that I had become more mature and thoughtful in spite of my suspected Americanization.

Papa had made the guest room into my room, closing it off with a curtain across one end of the room for privacy. He had converted the *tokonoma* (special display space) into a closet space for my clothes by running a hanging rod. He even added a small bed with a rose-colored futon cover that had been given to him for my use by one of his former employees.

Pilgrimage

The lovely room, I was told later by Aunt Fumiko, had been assembled at a great sacrifice, not only in expense but also in the strain that it had caused in Papa's home life. His wife had raised understandable objections to losing their guest room which had been the only unused space for their daily needs. Papa apparently correctly believed that during the long years of life in America I would grow accustomed to living in a separate room of my own. This was true and I welcomed the space.

As soon as all the fanfare died down, my quiet pilgrimage back to the Hiroshima I had left began. I took a small walk on the banks of the Ota river where I used to sit to watch the sunset and I visited the railroad crossing that had swallowed an old despairing man before my eyes. The four-leaf clovers were hard to find anymore. The dirt road along the river bank was more busily traveled; it was no longer a very restful place to sit in the hours of twilight as I had done in my youth.

MacArthur Road, which had seemed so needlessly wide when it was built during the American Occupation, seemed quite suitable now for the throughway it had become. Even finding my way back to the Yokogawa station, the nearest railroad stop, was awkward. The colors of the buses and the names of the bus lines had been changed and were completely unfamiliar.

The cafe called "The People's Hope" had moved to the downtown *Hon-dori* (Main Street), a fancier and more expensive section of the commercial district. Fukuya, the only department store in town now had a competitor, Tenmaya, a smaller store which offered less expensive items. The Main Street merchants pooled their resources to put a roofed cover over the walkways for all-weather shopping convenience much like an American shopping mall. It was the talk and pride of the town. I walked up and down looking for familiar landmarks and names. The bookstore Mama and I used to frequent during the war had been rebuilt but still occupied the same spot across from the Fukuya department store. The old established chinaware, kimono, and jewelry shops that used to be on Main Street before the war had been rebuilt in their former locations. The only change was that the shopkeepers now addressed me *oku-sama* (married female customer) rather than *ojo-sama* (unmarried younger female). To be accorded a title without having achieved such station in life was uncomfortable at first, but there was no point in calling special attention to my being a twenty-plus-year leftover *ojo-san* in a world where most of my friends had married and had growing children.

The Mission School buildings were being renovated but the senior high school was still in the structure that had been rebuilt immediately after the war. The students streamed out of school wearing the same uniform and school insignia showing no hint of the pain, hardships, or independent quest of our youth. I remembered when a small group of us, urged on by Ms. Jones, had marched into the faculty room to present our grievances. Though it had been unheard of for students to undertake such actions, the faculty members subsequently held discussion groups to hear more from the students and exchange ideas. The young girls before me now appeared well fed, well behaved, and content. The students on Mission College campus gave a similar impression. Their clothes were no longer threadbare nor their shoes worn down like many of ours once were. In the cafeteria a whale meat shish kebob prepared by the home economics students was being served to the staff and returning visitor. I had never tasted whale meat before. Apparently even the culinary tastes changed while I was gone.

The so-called epicenter was enlarged to make way for a peace park. The atom bomb museum had been completed since I had left, located not far from the memorial marker sculpted by Isamu Noguchi in the early years of the post-war period. Its engraved pledge, "The wrong shall not be repeated, so may you rest," seemed remote and powerless in a world so full of nuclear weapons.

The memorial dome was now fenced in so that no one could walk in and touch it. I remembered having sat on the rubble inside many times just to gaze at the broken-down walls and the burned steel structure. It was not quite the same to just look at it from outside the fence. It had become a symbol and a protected shrine while I was gone. I could not relate to a symbol I could not touch. As a youngster, I had little awareness of what I was actually trying to accomplish by going there, walking inside and climbing over the rubble. I even used to sketch the broken-down dome in watercolor. I wonder if it was because I had no other way of integrating or accepting my meager confrontation with the horrific destruction.

Having been away so long, and having studied many years to understand the grief of others, I thought I might gain profound insights as I paid homage to these markers of my youth. Instead, I felt uneasy and far less confident than I had anticipated. Could it be that nothing had changed in my life at a fundamental level? Or could it be that to relive so vividly my childhood memories of Hiroshima sucked out any feelings of confidence and security I had managed to develop?

I decided that I had to go back into another place in my past beyond Hiroshima, Kimita Village. It was there in the valley between the mountain passes on an early August day in 1945 that Miyoshi and I were compelled to beg our mothers to take us back home to Hiroshima. I had to see for myself if the village still existed in the same harsh conditions as when we had experienced it. Uncle I-chan and Papa agreed to drive. My stepbrother Hideo, Cousin Kumiko, and Little Cousin Toshie, Uncle I-chan's daughter, joined in the ride.

The trip from Hiroshima to Kimita, which took only a few hours by driving, had taken we Seibi children all day. It was a cool spring day. The flurry of wild flowers in pink, blue, and yellow covered the ground like beautiful carpets everywhere. I had never seen them before. The stream where we washed our faces and brushed our teeth had narrowed and become shallower but still flowed next to the rice paddies. I found the Zensho Temple just where I pictured it would be. The forty-some-odd stone steps were breaking down but an old woman who appeared at the gate invited us in. She was the mother-in-law of the young priestess with whom we gave daily sutra chanting. Did her son come home from the war? Yes, he did. Is her daughter-in-law still performing the temple duties? No, she has had children.

I asked her about one of the local village representatives who used to look after our needs. He had helped us to arrange places to bathe by persuading the farmer families to let us share in their facilities. She said that he died with an attack of appendicitis a few days after the Hiroshima bombing. The villagers carried him on a stretcher to a distant hospital in the town of Miyoshi. The doctor and the nurses were unable to get to him because of the huge number of dying atom bomb victims who had been transferred there. He suffered in pain, waiting for help that never came. The villagers had mourned for this kind and decent man. She said that they kept wondering why he had to die when his disease was so treatable. I could not have agreed with her more. Why, indeed? We continued bowing to each other as we parted.

I took my relatives back to my secret place of solace in the woods where a hanging bridge hovered over a fast-moving stream. The water was still breaking in an icy crystal splash as it moved over the large rocks under the bridge, but there was no longer any magic as we watched. I could almost hear the laughter of the Seibi children and feel the pure tranquillity that once was there. But now it was simply a clearing in the woods.

The village school still stood atop a small mountain with as many steps as before. The bars I had played on were exactly where they used to be. It was too cumbersome to explain to my family the taunting that followed after I had performed on the bar so many years ago. Remembering it vividly, I sought to find out what had happened to my one village friend who did not taunt me. Tracing my old memory we walked towards Takada's house behind the temple we had just visited. Amazingly the farm house was exactly as I had remembered it to be. It seemed to be a popular day for visitors at this farmhouse as a stream of people were going in and coming out.

There was no warning for the utter surprise that we would experience. First, a mature woman with a hand towel over her hair came towards us to see who we were. I recognized her face right away as that of my old friend's mother, who also remembered me from the days of our evacuation. She said that she had heard I had lost my mother in the bombing of Hiroshima. She also said that this was the day of the village council election and that her son was running for it. As we had walked up to the house, I had noticed several white flags planted in the ground, but I had not read the bold, black calligraphic letters on the flags. They were the words of encouragement for the candidate, Takada. However, I had not seen the phrase, written larger than life, the "Communist Party of Japan."

During the war, to declare one's affiliation with communism would have been a death sentence. Even in MacArthur's era many communist leaders had been purged. Membership in the communist party was not an easy political affiliation in a largely capitalist society nor for Takada, whose family appeared quite well off. Takada soon appeared, breaking away from his campaign crowd. I would not have recognized him from his sixth-grader days. He had grown tall and his fair and gentle face had turned to the darkest tan. If he hadn't smiled I would not have known it was the same person. His gentle eyes were stern and piercing with resolve. He chatted some and walked back as we bowed and I wished him good luck in his campaign efforts. I was jolted from nostalgia into the present, the changed today.

Cousin Kumiko remarked as we left the Kimita Village behind that it was not surprising for a young, serious, and idealistic man to turn to communism where local politics tends to be business as usual and young men are without a voice. Takada was always different from the rest. As someone whose kindness once saved my lost days, I hoped that his road ahead would be met with kind encounters. In the end, my Kimita Village no longer existed, even if the physical site of Kimita had not disappeared or been bombed as was Hiroshima.

At home I became more and more aware of the silence in our

household in contrast to that of my uncle and aunt with Cousin Kumiko. When I looked for the box in which I had kept my school pictures and yearbooks, art, and calligraphy that had won various awards, I learned that they had been discarded. The box had been moved out of the house to an outdoor shed where it had been exposed to rain and wind and eventually was thrown out. Aunt Fumiko who loved my brushwork retrieved one piece out of a large pile of weather-beaten photographs and papers. There was no explanation other than that the box had taken space that was needed inside. I regretted that I had not taken them with me.

It did not take me very long to realize that there was a void in our midst. All the theology and psychology courses and the field experiences I had behind me had not taught me how to fill this void. If there were a thousand oysters I would have opened them all to find one pearl that might have brought us closer.

My stepmother said that Papa was never talkative and he had had a frowning expression as long as she could remember. She added, "Except one morning, a few days before your arrival from America. He had walked outside after getting up and I saw him smiling and I heard him say, 'What a nice day.'"

I realized that I had become a stranger who could not be a part of the family without hurting the whole and this situation had created an extreme tension in the family. Finally one night, exhausted from the stress in the family my tears began to roll. My weeping turned to choking that continued through the night. I remembered then why so many years before I had once thought of going to the railroad to end my young life.

It was no one's fault. It was the evolution of broken pieces that could not fit together again. When the memories began to break through the denial that I had been using to protect myself, the buffer began to erode rapidly. The feelings of being abandoned and unsafe returned in full force. There in the middle of a pilgrimage back to Hiroshima, I found myself a helpless child who needed to flee again.

Uncle Hisao's swelling was now turning red and the surface of his skin was stretching and cracking after the radiation treatment.

The doctors were still uncertain about his problem and my uncle was left with the notion he had an incurable disease. In the old days, he used to joke about the shards of glass still under his skin in various parts of his body. They had been considered too risky to be removed and had been left there. After all of the other injuries he had suffered, these pieces of glass seemed to represent his invincibility in the past.

My uncle now joined others whose survival was ticking away with the clicking of an accelerated timer. None of us knew when, where, or how something would come over us. We did not know when we would hear the click of our own mortality and inevitably remember the sentence of the radioactive atom bomb that penetrated our flesh and the inferno we thought we had left behind. It wouldn't be over until the last breath we breathed.

Hiroshima Atom Bomb Hospital provided services to the ailing *hibakusha* free of charge. All *hibakusha* who could verify by witnesses that they had survived the bomb were eligible to receive a registration paper for free medical care and a few other care-related compensations. For those who had been under private care outside the national health care system like my uncle, the *hibakusha* registration card was of little use. To be on the safe side, I also received my survivor's registration paper upon my return home.

Having this paper was a double-edged sword: it provided an access to limited compensations but it also branded one as a *hibakusha*. The *hibakusha* were oddities from the beginning. No one knew how their bodies were changed. They died without any visible injuries in the early months of the post-war period. Then, an untold number continued to die slowly all throughout the province and elsewhere after they had relocated and presumably returned to normal health. An ominous cloud followed them as many complained of a malaise without a label. Rumors abounded that they were employment risks, for some failed to maintain steady work attendance. A possibility of increased birth defects as seen in the earlier days was no small cause of concern for the marriage brokers arranging candidates for matrimony. The business owners such as

my family and relatives had little to worry about in terms of
economic independence but I suspected that those without a solid
financial base would have had to try even harder to prove their
fitness to counter the public perception.

It appeared also that the *hibakusha* were reminders of a tragic
past that the country and the public—both in recovery—would just
as soon forget. The sentiment would have been echoed in some of
the *hibakusha* themselves. I didn't want to think about it, and I did
my best to run from it. But the peculiar cost of denial always follows
one. Mine was no exception. The past always catches up with us in
one way or another.

My former classmate Yoshino was also having difficulty with her
past catching up. We had both left Hiroshima the same year to
attend college. She had suffered earlier from a general malaise in
Columbus, Ohio, where she and her husband lived with a young
son. Doctors were unable to discover any cause for her symptoms
and attributed them to an adjustment problem. Finally, she traveled
back to Hiroshima and sought help from the Red Cross Hospital
where she was diagnosed as having stomach cancer. When I
returned to Hiroshima, she was convalescing after three-quarters of
her stomach had been removed. Her spirit was remarkably upbeat
in spite of the ordeal. Her American husband had joined her and
shortly thereafter they headed back to Columbus.

Although I was resigned by this time to the idea that I could not
stay in Hiroshima permanently, I was still determined to find work
in which I might utilize my education and training. I thought of my
grueling years in school, fighting fatigue, mental terrors, and the
persistent language barrier, in spite of the good will extended to
enable my education. I could not give up without at least trying to
help people in Hiroshima.

Only a few of my classmates who had not married yet were
pursuing career paths around that time. Social work was understood as volunteer charity work for the unfortunates. To find a
vocational opportunity that would allow me to give back what I had
learned was fast becoming doubtful. How well I had learned was
also in question judging from my lack of personal progress.

The notion of a woman being employed was not a comfortable one for my family even though they knew intellectually my education should be put to use. Papa's colleague, Mr. Matsuda, was willing to hire me as his personal secretary in the Mazda corporate office. I was no more qualified for that than I was for the next job offer working as a cottage mother for an orphanage. The job entailed all of the domestic and custodial care duties, taking care of ten to twelve children alone around the clock.

The Ministry of Welfare had not yet defined social work as a paid occupation, although an undergraduate college of social work had been established a few years before in Tokyo. Its graduates were establishing networking contacts but social work jobs were very scarce. Working as an interpreter or serving as a bilingual secretary were still likely job prospects for an American-educated female. I began to doubt if there was a place for me in Japan even vocationally.

During Billy Graham's spring crusade I had been invited to act as an interpreter for the Maebashi region. Hiroko, a fellow classmate from the Mission School who had been married to a Baptist minister, was receiving several Texas evangelists and needed an interpreter for their missions. I took the opportunity to join the team and to expand my job search at the same time, staying in the Tokyo region, unsuccessfully knocking on doors in both the public and private sectors. If there was not a place in the family, surely there had to be a place working outside the family. However, neither seemed likely by this point. The remaining option was for me to return to the United States.

My former employer, Mrs. Frank Knight, known to her staff at the Chicago Child Care Society as Miss Ethel Verry, became quite sympathetic when she found out that I could not find a social work job. She began to inform the Immigration Office of her interest in my reentry as a desired and a needed professional.

Letters had been crossing frequently between Robert and me as we kept each other abreast of our experiences and plans, affirming our deep feelings. I looked for his letters like a soldier on the battle front starved for words of comfort. His was an untainted warmth that I believed would never be touched by my Hiroshima experiences. I still could not describe how empty and shattering my coming home had been, so I kept him from knowing the darkening shadows I was walking through at the time. Robert was not alone. I told no one about them. I had not understood or accepted them to be anything other than my own shortcomings. I was bent on keeping them to myself.

One day during lunch when Papa and I sat alone, I told him about my thoughts on the surface developments since I had come home. Neither of us spoke of the incredible hardships and the struggles that we continued to experience as a result of the bombing and the war. That was a given. It was something we all lived with, like living in the mud would be if one's designated dwelling place was in the mud. The mud would be taken for granted, not discussed. Venting regrets or questioning how life might have been under other circumstances were luxuries we seldom indulged in.

I also told him for the first time about Robert and me, how we had met, about the kind of a person he was, his many strengths of character, and about our love for each other. I described his academic track, his continuing graduate work, and his interest in teaching political science. Papa was very quiet but listened intently. I could not tell from his immediate reaction whether he was relieved or disappointed that I had actually chosen a young man. I told him that ours was a long term commitment, that we had not set a timetable for our marriage, and that I hoped Robert felt very flexible about it as well. I believed that of all people, he would understand. He had once defied the code of his own society when he chose to marry my mother.

He looked at the large black and white portrait photo of Robert for a long time. He spoke with deliberation. He said that he would miss me if I were to leave again but he would try to support my decision. He said he would need to talk it over with Uncle Hisao and others of the family for their consent in the decision. Aunt Fumiko was saddened and tried to suggest I stay on. Why did I have to leave in so short a time she pleaded. Uncle Hisao was also averse to my leaving, siding with my aunt. Papa gave the situation a romantic twist by asking them to bless young love. In the end they gave in to Papa's wish to let me go.

As soon as the news of my interest in leaving the country became known, the tension in my immediate family became less apparent. I knew then, painful as it was, that I had made the right decision. An unmatched piece of the puzzle was removing itself, gravitating towards yet another pilgrimage.

14

Farewell, Hiroshima

Separation

Ms. Verry's persistence paid off, and the papers for my reentry were put together within a period of several months. Robert's letter conveyed his enthusiasm for my early return. The Tamura clan gathered again at the Hiroshima station to see me off, just as it had a little over a decade ago. It was quite different for me this time. I was leaving with the realization that I had been unable to confront the dark side of my Hiroshima. Nothing had been solved for me.

I was leaving feeling more shattered and less worthy. The hope of reaching my expectations seemed impossible whether I was in or out of Hiroshima. The broken pieces were like the rubble in the ruins of my late grandfather's once grand estate. They needed to be cleared before a new structure could be built, no matter how small or humble. I tried to tell myself that a new trial compelled by past failures has to be an essential step in any discovery. The often heard remarks made by my former clients returned with a fuller meaning as they used to say, "I'm sick of trying any more."

Thinking about this did not silence my disappointments or provide any energy to pack my bulky collection of belongings. Papa helped by constructing boxes with plastic lining. He was trying to start up a new business in chemical coating while helping his ailing brother with sewing needle manufacturing. It was a difficult time for everyone.

A small dinner party was organized at the suggestion of Aunt Fumiko. For the last time, she cooked a festive red snapper with thin Japanese noodles. Trendy French dishes were prepared by Cousin Kumiko and meat dishes with finely prepared salads were added by my stepmother. Aunts Kiyoko and Shizuko joined together and spoke into a microphone for the first time in their lives to record their parting wisdom. Cousin Kumiko sang a theme song from the popular TV program, "Let Us Meet in Our Dreams." Uncle Hisao, too, belted out some ancient Chinese poetry even with his swollen neck. We chanted along with him. Their voices still echo in my ears when I think of that afternoon. They must have sensed that I knew that this journey was different from the last one I had taken many years before. They must have known that they might be gone before the next reunion. We told each other just the opposite. The World's Fair would be on and the Olympics, and of course, they wanted me to come back with my husband.

I remember the sunny room where we sat and how I wished deep within that those happy moments might have been daily occurrences instead of the parting event. How easy it might have been to say that I had changed my mind, had there been laughter and smiling faces earlier even with all the nightmares of Hiroshima. But it was not to be. The permanent changes brought on by the consequences of war had to be lived with. I wanted to go as far away from Hiroshima as I could. I would find my work and home in Chicago with Robert.

The Tamura clan congregated on the platform of the Hiroshima Station before the train pulled out. Unlike the vibrant first journey my voice cracked and turned into silent tears as I thanked my relatives for their coming. Papa and my stepmother accompanied me on this journey to Tokyo where I would fly off to America again.

I can only remember the rapid climb of the jumbo jet when it took off from Haneda Airport. I knew this was to bring a termina-

tion of my past relationship to Hiroshima. I cannot remember how
we parted at the airport. I do remember treating Papa and my
stepmother to a steak dinner the night before in Tokyo. I can still
see their faces in the lighted candle. Papa had taught me how to
dine in European style when I was a small child. He took us to a
very auspicious looking dining room in a hotel on Miyajima Island.
He pointed to an array of silverware, and their respective uses for
soup and salad, meat and fish, holding the fork in the left hand
without changing it to the right hand as we progressed through
several courses of food. The scene came back to me as I watched
him and Tetsuko-san enjoy their last meal with me.

I do remember how it felt to step on San Francisco soil when the
plane finally landed there after a brief stopover in Honolulu. Arlene,
a classmate from McCormick, was there to help usher me back into
the country. I have no recollection of the details except for a great
sense of relief to find that there was indeed a place to which I could
return where I might resume my work life and personal growth in
my committed relationship with Robert. Such was my plan, and I
did not doubt that it was the best course that I had chosen.

What I did not know when I walked out of the gate at O'Hare
Airport was that I had returned a changed person, having intensely
relived the shadows of my life. The beaming face of Robert came
into my vision immediately. Robert eagerly embraced me and
planted a long kiss. It was then that I knew something was terribly
wrong. I wanted to push him away. My conscious thought was that
this was not the Japanese way. It is not correct to be so publicly
demonstrative. But I also felt lifeless inside. Collecting my thoughts
I recalled how much I had loved this person standing before me,
and though I could recall these feelings, the actual excitement was
gone.

My apprehension was detected by Robert, who was not given to
be an aggressive inquisitor. I overrode my discomfort and continued to reply that there was nothing wrong with me whenever
Robert asked. In a few short weeks he was to return to his parents'
farm in Idaho and then go off to Seattle, Washington, for his
continuing studies. We decided that I would join him sometime

later after I served for a sufficient period in the agency which had invited me back.

As I look back, I recognize how idealistic and impractical we had both been to have given ourselves so short a time to become readjusted to one another. I had just severed my ties, at least temporarily in my mind, to the country of my origin and to my family. I was feeling numb and separated from all close ties. The numbing effect did not discriminate. I felt distanced from Robert just as I felt distanced from everyone else. Perhaps it was even more scary with Robert whom I had loved. I had come to recognize more than ever the folly of human love, because it was subject to change and could even be left unrequited by death. I needed space to regroup myself from the Hiroshima memories. I may have returned with something akin to combat fatigue but with a resolve to keep out any further demands. Confused, I wrote to Robert to discuss our commitment at the end of that summer.

On the Labor Day weekend of that fall, I flew to Spokane, Washington. In a small cafe just across the Canadian border, I suggested that we break our engagement. Our eyes were red as he drove his father's DeSoto on a scenic highway. I tried to explain in the best way I could that I was having problems with feelings and he was not to be faulted. Robert had already sensed my reservations earlier and did not question my explanations other than to assume that I had a change of heart. (Neither of us had heard about Post Traumatic Stress Disorder such as experienced and described in later years by the Vietnam vets.) Robert wanted me to keep the set of rings he had given me. He said that his heart was with me and that I might as well keep them for him. I walked through the vacant airport in the dark hours of the night when I returned to O'Hare. Something inside felt like a lone kite floating with a string held by no one.

The correspondence between us became less and less frequent until one day a letter from Robert arrived requesting a return of his rings. There was no explanation. It was not necessary. Just as he did not ask any questions in the little border cafe, I assumed that his love had finally died. I had thought that all love eventually would.

Search

Suffering from something like the combat fatigue experienced by former veterans who disappear into the woods and mountains, I buried myself in human services. Mine was a mission of seeking peace of mind while serving the needs of my young and old clients. My work of counseling young mothers and finding homes for the abandoned was taken just as seriously as if they had been my own problems. Ms. Verry/Mrs. Frank Knight and the Chicago Child Care Society where I stayed ten years saw me through my early struggling years in the helping profession.

Festive dinners on holidays and tantalizing fresh fish and seafood every Friday could be counted on at the home of Frank and Ethel Knight. Usually very sharp and articulate, Mrs. Knight would never contradict her brilliant, but nevertheless, opinionated husband. She would simply remark in a gentle protest, "Why, Frank!" and Dr. Knight would chuckle. I could not have been in more agreement with Dr. Knight, however, when he would comment, "The human race is rotten," usually speaking of human strife in the world. It was my sentiment exactly. As the founder of the Chicago School of Economics, he helped produce several Nobel Prize–winning economists. Dr. Knight was a humble and congenial host always.

My growing interest in the counseling field led me to enter psychoanalysis as a prerequisite to training. After working four years with Dr. Joel Handler I was able to accept and enter a marriage that would last twenty years and to receive the remarkable gifts of a daughter and a son. Though enduring in years, the marriage was fraught with the markers of my Hiroshima experiences. Terrorizing images returned frequently including the simulation of death during work hours or at home no matter how hard I worked to eliminate them. Even the images of the clawing hands over the Gate of Hell appeared strongly and frequently.

They emerged while I was working with a noted psychiatrist, Milton Erickson in Phoenix, Arizona, who taught and utilized hypnosis in his therapy. His suggestion that I go deep into hypnosis and return to a happy part of my childhood left me cut off from my actual Hiroshima experiences much to my great delight. My chest would feel a warmth each time a hint of war memories returned.

Unlike the previous headaches or nausea, this was a far easier response. But a few hours later I would start to see from the corner of my eyes countless hands moving and crawling over an iron gate. They would not go away. At least the headaches always stopped. Without further instruction from Dr. Erickson I climbed a nearby hill, named Squaw Hill, at a predawn hour as if following my instinct for survival. I had not been prepared for a rough climb but I chose scaling rather than taking a path. Bruised and scratched I made it to the top after which the image disappeared. It was then, I realized that Hiroshima would be with me always.

Another time of discovery came while working in a training seminar with Dr. Kubler-Ross. My request to work on my grief led to a private session with one of the trainers who insisted on my verbalizing what I had not uttered at the moment of the atom bomb explosion. After repeated protest on my part that a Japanese individual may be incapable of such an expression and her refusal to accept my reservation, I heard myself call out, "Mama, I am so scared."

It may be ridiculous to say that what I heard was a discovery, but it was my first admission to myself that the deafening sound of explosion and the raging motion of destruction took away even a small opportunity to ask for my mother's help that I had truly needed at that moment. Unfortunately, my subsequent physical reaction of profound nausea and headache resulting from it recurred each and every time I spoke about my Hiroshima experiences after that. I simply had to become silent on the subject.

My search also took me to Toronto where Dr. Fennigstein, a Holocaust survivor of the Polish Ghetto where he was a physician, conducted workshops for survivors. I gained a profound insight into the similarities in the aftereffects of survivorship between my experience and those of the Holocaust's survivors. Just as remarkable a set of similarities appeared in what the survivor parents tended to seek in their children; survivor parents tended to place greater than normal expectations on their children. It was a profound wake-up call for me as a mother. The births of my healthy children had brought me the utmost joy and highest hope and had put to rest the fear of anomalies in *hibakusha* offspring. They were more than normal, being beautiful and spirited from the start. There was no room for taking time just being childlike for the children of the survivors. I had always expected so much more from my children than they had been ready for at their age. I could hardly wait to come home to enjoy the child in my children when I left Toronto.

By far the most significant help I received was from the work of Dr. Robert J. Lifton who chronicled the experiences of the Hiroshima survivors in his book, *Death in Life*. I was able to share the benefits of my understanding with Papa when he came to Chicago to be at my wedding. I told him about how important it was for us to be able to talk about our experiences. I told him about the concept of "psychic numbing," and said that if he had felt numb in all of what he had to do clearing the dead and searching for Mama, it was not because he was heartless as he might have thought. I told him about the tainted feelings of guilt that survivors often experienced for having survived while being powerless to save others. The man who taught me to walk, read, write, and paint artfully was now listening to me, taking in all that I could explain. We went on to talk for hours.

It was then that Papa told me about an encounter that he had not shared with anyone before, an encounter with a young American prisoner of war. Papa was at his Inland Sea Transportation head-quarters by the Ujina Harbor at the moment of the bomb explosion. He saw the flash and saw the buildings shatter, but he and his staff were unharmed. The first order was to survey the damage but the reports he received were so unclear he decided to investigate the situation himself. He was driven in a tri-motorbike by a staff driver. Collapsed houses and injured survivors overflowing the streets made the going extremely difficult.

About an hour or two into the surveying efforts, he spotted a group of people composed mostly of elderly men and women carrying stones in their hands and surrounding a tall, naked foreigner. He said that the young man was blue-eyed and blond, looking no more than about seventeen years old. Papa immediately surmised that this was an American prisoner of war who had wandered off and been stopped by the confused and understandably upset citizens. Papa got off the motorcycle seat to intervene. In his officer's uniform he spoke to them saying that the prisoner was obviously unarmed and not about to harm anyone, and that he was under the army protection. Papa stressed that they should not harm him. He directed the driver to escort the young man, and returned him to the barracks. As Papa described the young boy he even remembered the print on his boxer shorts.

"*Kawaisoni* (a pity), he was just a boy." Papa's eyes were seeing the young man again through his sharp painter's vision. His eyes were watery as were mine.

"His parents probably never knew what had happened to him, did they Papa?" I thought of the category "missing" to which Mama had been placed in the record book of the Hiroshima casualties.

"So was this young man in theirs?" I asked.

"No, they probably had no way of knowing," Papa replied.

I wanted to know more about it. What Papa told me then was even more shocking. He said there were forty to fifty prisoners of war who had been housed in the bunker at army headquarters near the Hiroshima Castle. Few survived the explosion. He went on to explain that during the clean-up operation while the citizens' bodies were being collected and cremated, he had given an order for burial rather than cremation for the American prisoners. He told his subordinates that this was the custom of the country from which they had come. My father, by granting the American dead their last respect in death, thus transcended all prior animosities. He said that the prisoners were buried along the banks of the Ota River near the dome. I was speechless as I thought about my father keeping this memory to himself.

A short time after my father's return to Hiroshima I was surprised to hear of his discussions with reporters about the

American prisoners of war who had died and were buried in Hiroshima. He even appeared on television when he identified the place where he and his men buried the prisoners. It was good for the citizens to know that our fate was shared. It was good for Papa to unload his untold sorrow.

Thus came the turning point for both of us in viewing our Hiroshima experiences from beyond the bonds of our own perspectives. Moving on with perseverance alone was not enough. In this Dr. Lifton's work helped us immensely. Long years of struggle were far from over but once in a great while there were moments in which I could become aware of the dimension of human existence even in Hiroshima experiences. Out of these feelings I wrote a poem of my struggle:

The Dawn

Towering and forbidding
was the gate before me.
Pounding and pleading
was my cry,
"But I need her, I need her, *now.*"
"The dead mustn't be disturbed child, run along *now.*"
Echoed the wall.
"If she can't come, take me to her, let me pass."
No more echo,
no more.

But for my bruises,
and torn flesh,
no one heard
no one saw.

A score of years I ran,
behind me crumbled the wall
slowly disintegrating into pieces so small.
"You may return now,"
the voice was heard in the wind.
"You'll see our monuments,
upon them you'll build Your City,
find your roots in the ashes of your parents,
shelter your love in the rubble of their dreams."

So the children who survived
because they could run,
returned as men and women
to the site of tomorrow.
One lighted a torch,
it burned so quickly
he was frightened.
Another searched for water,
but the earth was dry.

They huddled in the cold
as the night pierced
through their shivering limbs.
Their pilgrimage into the past
for the sake of tomorrow
ended for many before the dawn
when the morning sun
could have brought moisture and warmth.

I think I was lucky, I waited.

My professional career involved moving on from child welfare
into the mental health field working as a supervisor in a psychiatric
clinic within a university medical school. My knowledge base and
skills training were expanding further. After the arrival of my two
children I worked my own hours in private practice so that I could
spend more time with my young children.

It was through watching and experiencing their growing years
through my children's eyes that I became more thoroughly edu-
cated to what it is like to grow up in American society. These years
were exciting beyond imagination and at times tormenting like no
other. The abundant resources stimulated the birth of many talents
in Miko and Joshua, helping them to stretch their potential. They
also suffered the downside of being different from others, at times
being taunted and at times hitting a glass ceiling where abilities
were secondary to the color of their skin.

When I enrolled my two children in a laboratory school of a
university thirty-five miles away from our house, I decided to work
on the university campus during their school hours to help with

their travel. Little did I realize then that I was opening another door of discovery for myself. The work was tedious in the beginning, especially since I had never worked in a hospital setting. Being a *hibakusha*, the future state of my own health was uncertain, therefore, I preferred not to be reminded of sickness, particularly cancer from which a disproportionately high number of *hibakusha* were still dying.

So it was an awesome encounter in one of my early assignments in the organ transplant service to meet patients in critical care hooked to a multitude of mechanisms for life support. As I came closer to give words of encouragement, a most healing warm thought suddenly occurred to me that everything medically and humanly possible was being done for these patients, and that I could now participate finally in the same effort.

Long ago in another time, the bodies lay without care, medicine, food, or even water. The whispering sound of people in agony had not left my memory. I had had no water to give, nor presence of mind enough to know how to comfort anyone. Here in another time, participating in life-affirming efforts with the best medical support had become possible.

When an opening came up to provide services to women suffering from cancer, I accepted the challenge despite my long-standing fear of the disease. My patients' amazing courage and resilience in confronting their life threatening illnesses brought me back again to Hiroshima. My classmate Yoshino, who died within two years of her surgery but had remained strong and hopeful, had to leave her little boy, just as some of the women I was seeing had to do also. Life has to move on beyond the profound grief experienced by all in one way or another.

An opening in the radiation oncology department was my final challenge. The massive machinery used to give treatment and to save lives was located in the bottom level of the hospital. The mere size of these metal structures was oppressive and intimidating. A part of me wanted to run, because I wanted no part of it, but the rest of me demanded the final confrontation with the very power source that had changed my entire life and my world. So that was how I had come to learn about the miraculous ability of radiation, discovered long before the atom bomb, to cure, to save, and possibly to extend lives rather than destroy and take them away. Being authentically present in the lives of patients at a life-threatening juncture, helping tackle whatever needs there may be, affirming their worth and their courage as fellow human beings has given me immeasurable satisfaction. I considered it a privilege to be there as we journeyed together.

As I worked with the oncology patients, I received invaluable help from a noted psychologist, Ken Moses of Evanston, and his team of trainers in grief counseling. One morning near the end of our training which had been started several months earlier, I asked to work on the very last unfinished piece of my grief: to discuss with Mama what I did not get to share with her or ask her after she waved good-bye for what we had both thought would be a brief parting nearly fifty years ago. The competent staff with authentic empathy and skills had won my trust and the trust of the group.

I heard myself asking Mama if she had suffered great pain and saying that had I known where she was I would have been there to dig her out at any cost, that I might well have died with her. The life that followed without her had felt unbearable and difficult. I recalled my wandering through dying people trying desperately to find her. I asked her if she could hear me in the wind as I had tried to comfort her the best I could, humming her favorite songs. I needed to know, Did you hear me, Mama? I apologized from the very bottom of my heart telling her how very sorry I was to have insisted on coming home the day we did when she would rather have stayed in the country one more day.

I took her through the markers of my life. I told her how sick I had become after the bomb but then when I was better, how hard I had tried to be an excellent student just as she had always wanted me to be. And that when I had achieved it, no one seemed to care, for no one came to see me receive the awards. It hadn't mattered to anyone but you, Mama. I told her that I lost my motivation after that but I kept on trying. I said how proud she would have been with her beautiful grandchildren who are growing into remarkable adults. I told her about the scary times I had encountered throughout my life and my attempt to protect the children against harm. The fear of my immune system failing while carrying on without the help of my family, I told her, had always been in the back of my mind. I also shared happy developments in my life.

It was a completion of grief work which would not have been possible without the authentic presence of Gwen, the sole female staff person on the team. The skills training that I undertook to better serve my patients was a gift that enabled me to validate my shattered dreams.

After the Rain

In the early summer of my daughter's senior year in high school, I became a single parent. A union which had begun with deep caring had slowly disintegrated into an abyss of exhaustion. The old wartime motto, "Do not ask until victory," had long left a conditioning in me to be quiet about my wants and needs until there was no more left to give. It was a painful, devastating time of separation. In the dark hours of my adulthood, the last wall of denial had to be faced as it came crashing down. It was as if I had come to the edge of a cliff, an infinite fall awaiting me.

In letting go of this abyss and entering solitude, I began to reconstruct the way I had been a long time ago, in a world safe, sound, and nurtured. I began to discover the boundaries and the passageways that had been stripped away from my childhood scarred by the horrific events in the history of our time. From the edge of the cliff I was to fly instead of falling.

I remembered my mother, who, though she died young, had been with me all along. I saw her courage in my own ability to move onto a rebirth, even without a promise or guarantee that the next stage would be better. In letting go, a lasting affirmation came through. It was not temporary this time.

I was then able to face the abysses squarely, to describe or possess or disown them freely. For I had finally discovered that the house in which I dwell is inside me. My home was built long before my physical world had been lost. A peace of mind, as never experienced before, evolved and the cup was finally full. I began to collect these memories without the fear of malaise that had so often plagued my past attempts at recollection. The collection of memories became this chronicle, titled *One Sunny Day*.

About three years into my single parenthood, my son happened to express an incidental thought, "Mom, I really miss having a male mentor." Although the thought of coupling again was incredibly remote, it prompted a nostalgic recollection of a few honorable individuals that I had known. The man to whom I had been engaged nearly thirty years before came easily back to my mind. I had mailed a Christmas card addressed to his parents' home in Idaho, hoping it would be forwarded. When it was returned marked "addressee unknown," I considered it a lost connection without giving it any further thought.

Two years later, I found myself resting in bed one April morning fumbling with a remote control for something on the television to distract the discomforts of a minor cold when suddenly a flashing ad on a talk show caught my eye. The ad invited the viewers with a lost love to write in and the TV show would try to find the individual. Considering this to be all in fun, I took down the information. Later, I sent in a brief description of how Robert and I had met at the International House of the University of Chicago in our student days. I spoke of our engagement and separation after my return from Japan. I added that I wanted to explain to Robert why I had broken the engagement.

About ten days later I was astounded to receive a phone call from the producer of the Hollywood program informing me that my friend Robert had been found in Alaska. A series of long letters and phone calls from Alaska began to reach me. Three dozen roses that arrived on the anniversary of Hiroshima were particularly beautiful. Salmon caught in the Alaskan sea and smoked locally arrived more than once. We slowly began to trace each other's lives and discovered that the bond that had brought us together more than thirty-one years ago was still very strong. Robert went on to say that there had not been a day that he had not thought of me in one way or another since our parting. We spoke on the phone daily, discovering how much common ground we still shared and being amazed by our similar outlook and philosophy. In the end it was Robert's decision to leave Alaska to fulfill our earlier broken dream of spending our lifetime together, a dream that had been shattered by my Hiroshima experiences that neither of us had questioned or understood at the time.

A year after our rediscovery of each other, we met at O'Hare Airport in Chicago for the first time in thirty-two years. I saw Robert emerging from the accordion wing breaking into a familiar broad smile, looking older with deeper facial lines and graying hair.

"Hi, Honey!" he exclaimed.

The sound of his voice was just as fresh as if he had just returned to the days of his youth. Our eyes met and we were back in time where we had begun in a small auto parked on a driving test site on the far south side of Chicago.

My long search for the authentic encounter brought me back to my former love. It was like coming home after a long detour. One morning after a brief New England rain shower, Robert and I exchanged long-delayed marriage vows in a small chapel at my daughter's college. The ceremony would have been held out of doors in the stunning campus site called, "The Biblical Garden" but the rain had sent us inside.

After the ceremony, we walked out onto the chapel steps where the sun was shining. On another sunny day I had found my full life again.

Epilogue

A few blocks away from my work place is a sculpture by Henry Moore titled *Nuclear Energy*. I had always loved his creations with the exception of this particular work. The massive round form reminds me of the mushroom cloud that once engulfed my hometown. It still intimidates me.

Recently, however, I found myself confronting all that the sculpture represents head on. I was stopped in a hallway of the hospital by a senior physicist in my department. I had seen him many times before and we usually exchanged cordial acknowledgment. On this occasion he ventured more. He said that he had come across an article taken from my memories of Hiroshima, then he remarked with a thoughtful expression on the more pertinent connection he had had with me. He said he had worked on the Manhattan Project. His role in Los Alamos had been to design the radar mechanisms that triggered the explosion at the exact point in the air that would be most effective. Stunned, my automatic reply was that the invention had indeed worked perfectly as the experience of our city would attest to.

Yes, he said, the chance of failure had been projected at one in a million. He added that he truly believed that the nuclear bombs hastened the end of the war thus saving more lives. He agreed with me that we could not relive history so we cannot know what might really have happened, and the historians' debate may go on indefinitely. The real point in talking about the subject at all for me, I said, was my concern for the world of today and tomorrow in which the concepts of enemies and "worthy" causes are murky and diverse. The question of who will have nuclear weapons and who may use them has become unclear. In sharing my own story, I said, I hoped to promote continuing reflection on the subject.

Many years ago I would not have been able to involve myself in such a dialogue as this. I would have become terrified by the appearance of someone who made the bomb happen. It still felt a bit strange, but the physicist and I shared very common ground today as we wished for a bright future for this planet.

As for our original *hibakusha* household, only Cousin Kumiko and myself remain. Shortly after my return to the United States, Uncle Hisao's malignant tumor metastasized to his brain. He suffered interminable pain the last six months of his life, with no adequate means to lessen his suffering. Aunt Yoshiko who was not a *hibakusha*, but whose live snapping turtle contributed to my recovery from the A-bomb sickness following the end of the war, died from grief and heart failure shortly after Uncle Hisao's departure. Aunt Kiyoko followed a similar path one evening shortly after bathing.

My late grandfather's manufacturing company that Uncle Hisao presided over and my father tried to help with, never quite recovered. The plant that suffered a second disaster by fire was reconstructed but never recouped its losses. Papa's new venture in a chemical coating for roofing and water proofing did not take off in his lifetime. He was a doting grandfather to my children, though he never got to see them or hold them in his arms. He died a few days after he wrote to me about how very tired he had come to feel every day. He was in his early sixties.

Widowed Aunt Fumiko lived alone until a stroke left her confined to a wheelchair. She was placed in a nursing home owned and managed by Cousin Kumiko and her physician husband. Aunt Fumiko passed away in her early seventies, the only one to live past her sixties in our *hibakusha* household.

During our time together, we never spoke among ourselves of our hardships or how our loved ones had died, except for the one conversation I had with Papa. We held a memorial service every year in August. From time to time some small thing would remind us of those who had perished from the A-bomb. We would then mention the happy times we spent with them and remember the promise and the dreams that they had had.

Perhaps the Hiroshima memories now buried deep in the hearts of *hibakusha* still make us want to cry out, "Mama, I'm scared."

Glossary of Japanese Words

ama-do: Rain door. Wooden sliding doors used to close in the house where there are no walls, keeping out the elements at night, or in extreme weather conditions during the daytime.

appappa: Plain, simple cut, loose-fitting, one-piece summer wear worn at home by women.

Astrakhan: Lamb's fur from the Astrakhan region of Russia or fabric imitation of the fur.

banzai: Cheers, as in "Long live the Emperor," or "Hip, hip hurrah," with both arms raised above the head.

bento **lunch:** Box lunch.

bura-bura: Being idle, aimless, and at loose ends.

Buraku-min, Buraku: The "Tribal People," referring to the ethnic minority known historically as "meat eaters" prior to the introduction of the Western dietary style. Due to religious prejudice against the Buraku and Buraku-min practice, the group suffered long-standing discrimination in social acceptance.

butsuma: A room reserved for the Buddhist altar used for religious worship *daikonoroshi*: Grated white radish, served by itself as a condiment or with broiled fish/seafood.

Edokko: Persons born and raised in Tokyo, the city formerly, called, Edo.

Fukushima-cho: A district in Hiroshima which had a high concentration of Buraku residents.

Fukuya: The first major department store built in Hiroshima at the gate of the main street.

genkan: The formal or front entrance to a residence.

getta **sandals:** Traditional wooden open clogs worn both by men and women of all ages. A pair of rectangular shaped wooden pieces are sanded and varnished. Thick wooden heels support the flat surfaced platform. Reinforced sandal strings come in colorful fabric for women and children.

go-between: A matchmaker in a matrimonial arrangement.

goshinei: The portraits of the imperial couple referred to as the "true shadows" of their majesties. The pictures were usually draped and hidden from direct eye contact by the commoners.

gunshin: Military saint. The term was accorded to those who sacrificed their lives with unprecedented courage and dedication in their service to the Emperor and their country.

gyokusai: Suicidal end in military defense or attack most frequently referred to during World War II.

hakama **wear:** Traditional skirt-pants worn over a kimono. Men and women frequently don them for traditional marshal arts exercises or other select occasions.

Hakata, port of: A coastal town at the northern tip of Kyushu Island, spared from the Mongol and Chinese invasion in 1274 and 1281 due to violent winds in which all the enemy ships were destroyed.

haori: Lightweight half-coat worn over a kimono tied in front by a set of decorative strings.

hibakusha: Atom bomb survivors. The literal translation is "person who was bombed" or "persons who were bombed."

Hon-dori: The name of the original downtown commercial district in Hiroshima. The literal translation is "the main street" or "the best street."

imon bukuro: A comfort/care package sent to soldiers at the battlefront.

itte kimasu: A customary greeting by a departing person who has the intention of returning, as in leaving for work or going to school.

Kabe: A small town north of Hiroshima. It is about a thirty-minute commuter train ride from Hiroshima.

kamikaze: Divine wind assisting patriots.

kanbu kohosei: Officer candidates. Military men without military schooling were able to pursue an officer's career by passing rigorous examinations and subsequent training.

Kasumigahara: The well known Japanese Air Force training base near the Tokyo region during World War II.

kenpei: Military police, an elite corps of military men engaged in security investigation and enforcement.

Kotohira: A town on Shikoku Island famous for the Konpira Shrine, the guardian of travelers.

Kure: A naval base east of Hiroshima.

kuro-chan: *Kuro* means black. *Chan* adds a tone of endearment.

Meiji Restoration: 1868 restoration of the imperial reign from the Tokugawa Shogun to the Emperor Meiji following a long period of civil war. It also marked the beginning of the westernization of Japan that ended 200 years of isolation.

Miyajima Island: A small island off the coast of Hiroshima, famous for its natural beauty and the Itsukushima Shrine, built in the twelfth century by Lord Taira, and is considered one of the three most scenic places in Japan.

mompe slacks: A government-designated wartime style of slacks resembling warm-up suits with an elastic bottom around the ankles. The women and school girls were required to wear them to show their patriotism.

mugikogashi: A sweet pudding made by mixing unrefined wheat flower and sugar in hot water.

namuamidabutsu: A prayer chant meaning "Save us merciful Buddha!" used in a context similar to the one for "May he rest in peace."

nemaki: A kimono worn for bed. Sleepwear usually made of a soft-textured fabric, like flannel or terry cloth.

obento lunch: Box lunch. Same as *bento*. An "o" affix does not change the meaning but softens the expression.

obi: A wide ornamental fabric belt worn over a kimono, traditional Japanese women's wear.

Obon: The Feasts of Lanterns— the Buddhist All Soul's Day. The lanterns are lit once every year on Obon evening for the souls of the deceased so they might find their way home and return to the beyond again.

ojami: Bean bags used in juggling games played by children.

ojii-chan: A term of endearment for "grandfather," as in "grandpa". *Chan* in Japanese after a name is an expression of affection.

ojo-sama: A respectable, unmarried young woman, or a daughter of a respectable family.

ojo-san: Same as *ojo-sama*, a young daughter. *Sama* connotes the expression of respect whereas *san* connotes endearment.

oka-san: Mother.

oku-sama: Madam. A term usually referring to a married woman or a female individual whose age appears to be past the teens or early twenties.

okyu: A traditional folk medicine in which dried moss is burned on designated parts of the body for the purpose of curing a variety of ailments.

omiai: A meeting of a couple arranged by a matchmaker for the purpose of exploring matrimonial interest.

oyobare: House dinner party.

pachinko: A children's game played by a collection of small reinforced picture cards. The object of the game is to flip or remove the opponent's cards by slamming one's own cards forcefully on the board without touching the opponent's cards.

pika-don: An audiovisual expression which Hiroshima survivors coined referring to the atom bomb explosion. *Pika* refers to the sudden flash and *don* refers to the sound of the explosion.

renpei-jo: Military training ground. There were East and West Renpei-jo in Hiroshima. The larger one of the two, the West training ground, adjoined the Seibi Academy.

saikeirei: The deepest bow reserved for the expression of deepest respect, appreciation and humility.

Sanzu, River of: The mythical water that must be crossed by the deceased to get to the world beyond. Similar to the River Styx.

Shikoku Island: One of the four major islands of Japan, southwest of the largest island, Honshu, facing the Inland Sea on the north and the Pacific Ocean on the south.

Shudo-In: The name of the orphanage located near the Hiroshima station. Atom bomb orphans and the Amerasian babies born during the Allied Occupation of Japan were being cared for in this institution. The literal translation of the name means, "Learning the Way."

tadaima kaerimashita: A formal Japanese greeting when one returns home. In daily and informal use, one may simply say, *tadaima!*

Takarazuka: A theatrical and musical training school for women, famous for producing Western-style musical revues. Established in the pre–World War II era, it continues to thrive through the present.

Takashimaya: A well known Japanese department store chain comparable to Bloomingdale or Neiman Marcus in the U.S. with international branches in Los Angeles and New York City.

Tenmaya: A competitor to Fukuya that was built during the post–World War II era. It sold lower priced and less exclusive items than those seen in Fukuya.

tatami: Floor mats made of fine reeds in a rectangular shape used to cover traditional Japanese rooms.

tokonoma: An ornamental alcove in a traditional Japanese sitting room or guest room, designating the center and order of the seating arrangement in which the host and the guest are expected to sit closest to the alcove.

Tomo: A farming village outside of Hiroshima.

Uebara: A farming community just outside the town of Kabe where much of the farming is done in the form of step-levels on hillsides and mountain slopes.

Yokogawa The second largest railroad station in Hiroshima. It is located in the northwest section of the city.

yoku kaetta: Welcome home.

yomise: A street market open usually in the summer nights, selling trinkets, goldfish, candies, and toys. The young and old cool off in their summer kimonos, fanning themselves and browsing through the vendors' booths.

yukata: A cotton kimono without a lining worn during summer evenings for cooling off.

zabuton **cushion**: A cushion used when sitting on a *tatami* mat.

zashiki: A drawing room or parlor usually facing the garden. Generally speaking, this room is reserved for receiving guests.

Index